# THE ROUND TABLE

How relational intelligence will become your human advantage in the AI age



Sarah Stone McDevitt

First published in 2026


ISBN Paperback: 978-1-7384262-8-7
ISBN Hardback: 978-1-7384262-9-4
ISBN eBook: 978-1-7384234-7-7



Published by Book Shelf Press, 2026
Editor: Ameesha Green
Proofreader: Gemma Rowlands
Project Manager: Niall Burgess
Typesetter: Kyle Albuquerque



www.thebookshelfpress.com

BOOK SHELF PRESS ®

*For my Aunt Tina and my dad,
who taught me the power of
human connection*

# TABLE OF CONTENTS

# AUTHOR'S NOTE

Let me be clear about this from the start: I used AI to help write this book.

I want to be clear about this because it would be daft to write a book about AI-amplified humans without demonstrating exactly how AI can amplify a human.

You see, writing a book would have been impossible for me just a few years ago. I have dyslexia–the kind where I can't see what letters words start with (called *phonological dyslexia*), and so I've spent my entire life knowing exactly what I want to say but struggling to get it onto the page. I've been living in a world where the pen was supposed to be mightier than the sword, but for me, the pen was a sword that I couldn't pull out from the stone.

And then, along came AI. Suddenly, there was an ally to help me say what I wanted to say. This is precisely what this book is about: using AI to amplify uniquely human capabilities, rather than replacing them.

Will my use of AI to write a book cause a debate? Probably. Does that bother me? Not in the slightest. Some people will feel that I have no right to write this book, that using AI is cheating. But AI didn't write my stories–I lived them. What AI did was help me overcome the barrier that had always stood between my stories, my ideas, and the world.

So yes, I used AI to amplify the writing in this book. This book exists precisely because I combined my human experience with AI to create something that neither of us could have achieved alone. I also worked with a human, neurodivergent book editor for the parts that humans do best. That's the future I'm advocating for–not humans versus AI, but humans working with AI.

You can decide whether the ideas and stories in these pages are worth amplifying and sharing with the world. But please don't judge the worth of the ideas based on the tool that I used to share them. Judge them based on whether they help you build better relationships and find that sweet spot where technology serves humans and helps us to flourish.

# INTRODUCTION:
## The Round Table

It was 1989, and I was eight years old when I learned something that would shape the rest of my life, though I wouldn't understand it for decades. It happened at the back of a classroom in a small school in Ireland, at a round table. This table was where the teacher had banished the children she deemed "not worth her effort".

We'd moved from a tiny two-room schoolhouse in Leitrim, where 45 students made up the entire school, to a bigger location where 45 students filled my class alone. The teacher had what she called a "progressive" approach to education, and she organised the classroom by ability. The brightest students sat at a triangle table near the front, with very sharp edges. The average students were at square tables in the middle, with just enough angles for them to handle. The rest of us–the misfits, the dreamers, the ones who didn't fit her mold–were exiled to a round table at the very back (I presume she thought we would hurt ourselves on tables with corners).

I remember the first Friday's spelling test like it was yesterday. I knew I was going to fail before we even started because I'm phonetically dyslexic. When the teacher called out the word "beautiful", I heard the sounds but couldn't connect them to the letters. I spent precious seconds just trying to figure out how to begin, while the triangle table kid was already moving on to the next word.

But what I remember about the round table was that the other kids sitting with me weren't stupid. Far from it. They were among the most interesting and intelligent people I'd ever met. They could tell stories that would make you cry with laughter. They noticed things about people that others missed. They had a way of connecting with each other that felt more real than anything happening at the front of the class.

I was confused. If these kids were so brilliant in their own ways, why couldn't the teacher see it? And why weren't they being heard?

That's when I learned my first lesson about human intelligence, and not the kind that shows up on tests, but the kind that actually matters in the world. This kind of intelligence helps you read a room, understand what someone needs, and make genuine connections with other humans.

I also learned something else at the back of that classroom: If I was going to make my way in the world, it would have to be with my voice, not with a pen. Even if the pen is mightier than the sword for some of us, the pen is stuck in the stone for others. But I could talk (I'm sure some people wished I would talk less, but that's another book), and more importantly, I could listen.

While the triangle table kids were busy memorising facts and formulas, us round table kids were learning to read people. We had to. We were the ones who didn't fit the system, so we had to figure out how to navigate it differently. We learned to pay attention to the things that textbooks don't teach, like the subtle shifts in tone that tell you someone's having a bad day, the way people's faces change when they're genuinely interested versus just being polite, the art of making someone feel seen and heard.

Maybe you were a round table kid too, maybe you have your own "round table" moment, or maybe you have a different origin story. Either way, the moral of the story is the same.

And this wasn't the first round table to teach people a similar lesson. In the legend of Arthur, a seemingly ordinary boy pulls a sword from a stone that nobody else can shift. This act reveals him as the rightful ruler, not through birth or wealth but through the strength of his character.

Later, when Arthur becomes king, he creates a Round Table to communicate with his knights. The table has no "head", and everyone seated there is equal. The table was a symbol of fairness, unity, and respect for one another, a collective intelligence, with each person bringing their unique strengths to create a better future.

While the teacher saw the classroom's round table as a place for the "less capable", it ironically mirrors that visionary table from legends past. It also shows us a path to the future.

In the age of AI, many of us are worried that it will take our jobs, that there will be no place for us. And so the story goes that AI is something to be feared or avoided. I am here to tell a different story. One where humans and AI can work together, where AI can amplify humans like me and you, where the power of human connection plus tech can create business intelligence. And it all starts with understanding human connection.

That's why this book starts with my personal stories, particularly those of my family growing up in Ireland, and my early lessons in communication. As the book progresses, we'll enter the workplace and explore the lessons in communication I learned there (though the businesses have been anonymised). Towards the end of the book, you'll find a practical tool I developed to help managers and companies navigate the age of AI: a compass of sorts based on a concept I call "relational intelligence". This progression from personal life to business life is intentional, and it reflects my lived journey of communication and human connection.

If you're wondering whether this book is for you, I wrote it for people who don't want to win at work by becoming less human. For those who want to work with AI rather than against it. Maybe you're a leader, a founder, or a knowledge worker who is seeing AI enter the playing field and aren't sure what role it, or you, will play moving forward. Ultimately, it's for any human who doesn't want to become a robot.

Of course, there will be those who disagree with my assessment of the playing field, those who think I am being naïve, and those who think we are all doomed. I prefer to be more hopeful, and my hope is based on a lifetime of seeing the power of human connection and relational intelligence in action. While I respect the value of considering risk and planning for worst-case scenarios, that is not the focus of this book. This book is here to provide a hopeful path forward.

# HUMAN CONNECTION | 1

The round table wasn't the first time or place where I had seen the power of human connection. I was surrounded by it in my family—who are very proud people that enjoyed debates, long stories, competitions, and empathy in equal measure.

I come from two families of farmers, and in that world, your word is your bond. You are always making deals, working with people, and building relationships that last for generations.

My grandfather had a test he'd use when hiring farm workers. He'd give them their lunch and observe how they ate. If they ate quickly, he'd hire them—he figured anyone who ate fast clearly had somewhere to be, and he hoped that was back to work. If they ate slowly, he'd assume they had too much time on their hands and wouldn't be hard workers. It sounds extreme, but he was always reading people, looking for signs of character and motivation that went beyond a CV (not that they had one in those days). He understood that hiring someone wasn't just about their skills but their attitude, work ethic, and ability to add to the team, or in this case, the family farm.

My grandmother on my mum's side was a district nurse who delivered babies, helped people die, and saw every shade of human experience in between. She could walk into a house and know within minutes what was really going on, not just medically but emotionally, socially, and spiritually. She had this gift for seeing the whole person, not just the problem they presented.

But it was my parents who really taught me about the power of human connection.

My father was a Garda. A police sergeant in a village called Manorhamilton. But he wasn't your typical by-the-book copper. His philosophy was simple: If you want to solve crimes, you need to understand people. And if you want to understand people, you need to genuinely care about them.

He spent his days checking on the senior residents in the village, not because it was required, but because he believed they were the connective tissue of the community. They were the ones who sat by their windows watching the world go by, who knew everyone's business, who could tell you exactly who was acting strange and when. They were, in his words, "the best intelligence network you could ask for".

Every Christmas, he'd throw a party for the older people in the community. He'd hire a band, organise food, and make sure everyone felt special. I used to think it was just him being nice, and I'm sure that was part of it, but I realise now it was strategic brilliance. He was investing in relationships that would pay dividends for years to come.

There wasn't a shop he went into where he didn't make eye contact with the person behind the counter, ask about their day, remember their family situations, or make a cheesy joke. He had this song he would hum just to get people's attention. As a kid, I was sometimes painfully embarrassed by his antics but also by how long these conversations took. We'd pop into the local shop for a loaf of bread and end up hearing about the shopkeeper's grandson's final exam results, her husband's arthritis, and her opinion on the new road works.

But those conversations were his real work. He wasn't just buying bread but maintaining a network of relationships that made his job possible. When something went wrong in the village, he didn't need to launch an investigation. He'd receive three phone calls telling him exactly what happened before the paperwork even crossed his desk. My father understood how the community worked, and he supported it every chance he could. In fact, my older brother Jim followed in Dad's footsteps and became a Garda too, and watching him take a similar approach to his work confirmed something I already knew–the uniform doesn't do the job, relationships do.

My mum was a nurse at Sligo General Hospital, working first in geriatric care and later in ear, nose, and throat. Like her mother, she had a remarkable ability to see past the medical condition to the person underneath. Mum spent extra time with patients who seemed lonely, remembered details about their families, and somehow always knew exactly what to say to make someone feel better.

I learned from both parents that the most important part of their jobs wasn't the technical stuff–it was the human stuff.

Dad could arrest someone, but the real skill was in talking them down, so arrest wasn't necessary. Mum could administer medication, but the real healing often came from the five minutes she spent just listening to someone's fears.

When adults came to our house for dinner, I'd find excuses to hang around the kitchen, desperate to hear their conversations. I wanted to understand the ebb and flow of adult interaction, the way people shared information, the subtle negotiations that happened in every exchange. I couldn't explain why, but I was fascinated by the mechanics of human connection.

Human conversation became my classroom. While other kids were struggling with books and essays, I was learning from the masters of relationship building who happened to be sitting at our kitchen table every Sunday.

I learned so much from the stories my parents told me around that table, about their experiences and the way they made decisions, not just using their heads but also their hearts, or what we call "value-based judgements" today.

Back in the 1980s in Ireland, there was an incident in our small town where a group of young men were caught stealing money. By the letter of the law, the right thing to do would have been for my dad to charge them with a crime. That would have been the straightforward, procedural path, the one that most people would have taken without thinking twice.

But my dad saw something more than the mistake. He saw the people behind it, young men who had made a bad choice, but whose lives could still take a very different course if given the chance. He also understood the consequences. A criminal record would have meant they could never get a visa to travel to America, in 1980s Ireland with high unemployment it would have cut off opportunities that might change their futures.

So instead of pressing charges, he called in their parents. He told them what had happened and laid out a different kind of justice. The boys would work over the summer to repay every penny they had taken. They would publicly apologise to those they'd wronged and make amends. It wasn't easy, it was humbling, uncomfortable, and hard work. But it was also redemptive.

Years later, a now grown man stopped my father on the street and said, "You won't remember me, but I'll never forget what you did. I live in the States now, I've built a successful business, a family, a good life. None of that would have been possible if you hadn't given me another chance."

That moment has stayed with me my whole life. It taught me that true leadership isn't about blindly following process or policy but about judgement, empathy, and courage. It's about choosing the path that serves people, not just rules.

My dad understood something that's even more relevant in today's world of automation and digital systems: Not every decision can be made by logic alone. Sometimes, the human thing to do isn't the easiest or the most defensible on paper. But it's the thing that changes someone's life.

Outside of the family dynamic, the same story also played out. I'm a social creature, so wherever there are people, I want to be there and observing interactions. As a teenager, I played football, and I wasn't particularly good at it but I loved listening to the older women on the team talk about their lives, challenges, and dreams. They taught me things no textbook could about resilience and juggling multiple responsibilities while retaining their human connections.

I also worked dozens of jobs: at bakeries, factories, radio stations... anywhere people gathered and talked. Each job was like a masterclass in human behaviour and communication. I learned that every workplace has its own social dynamics, unwritten rules, and way of deciding who gets heard and who gets ignored.

At those workplaces, I loved watching the people who were genuinely skilled at human connection. They all had something in common: They were genuinely curious about other people, just like I had seen with my family. They asked questions not to fill the silence, but because they truly wanted to know the answers. They remembered details about people's lives. They showed up when it mattered.

When I was seventeen, I joined the Reserve Army. You might think military service would be all about following orders, but it taught me something different: People don't follow orders just because they're told to. They follow orders from people they trust, people they believe care about them, people who have earned their respect. Again, it was about building connections, and knowing how to communicate.

As it happens, I was in the Communications unit (known as the signals unit), which was all about communication. But the real communication lessons came from working in a team of people from different backgrounds, socioeconomic levels, life experiences, and perspectives. There, I learned that effective communication isn't about having the right words but understanding the person you're talking to well enough to know what words will land with them. (Although there are some words we can all get united behind, like "DUCK!")

Through these experiences, I figured something out early on: The people who could communicate effectively and connect were almost always the most successful, regardless of their technical skills. Success by one measure is about career, sure, but it's also about motivation and satisfaction. They were the ones who got promoted, built things, and created opportunities for themselves and others. All because they had figured out something that the education system doesn't teach you: Success isn't just about what you know–it's about how well you connect with those around you.

I didn't have a name for it back then, but I was seeing the power of what I later coined *relational intelligence*. And it wasn't the only time I saw it.

# BETWEEN THE LINES | 2

Growing up in Ireland in the 1980s, if you wanted to talk to someone, you had to work for it. And not just because I'd have to fight my younger sister Jane for the phone. If you were lucky, you'd ring them on the phone attached to the wall in the hallway, arrange to meet up, and spend time together without seven other conversations happening simultaneously on your devices. If you were unlucky, you'd sit in a car by the side of a country road while your mother worked her way through her phone book on the local pay phone.

It was inefficient as hell. But that inefficiency created something: the conditions for real conversation. Being stuck to that wall or that payphone meant no distractions, purely listening to the other person, seeing where the conversation goes. And the fact that you had to work harder to speak to someone, and wait your turn to use the phone, meant you valued the conversation.

When we finally got a phone in the house, it was closer to the mid-90s. When my friend Niamh called to tell me about her breakup with that *eejit* Declan, we spent two hours on the phone, most of it wandering through seemingly unrelated topics: school, her family, what she was reading, what she was worried about. By any modern efficiency metric, 80% of that conversation was "unnecessary". But all of it was necessary for the relationship, and we didn't exchange key information points optimised for call duration. Although my father was often unconvinced it was necessary when the phone bill came.

Those long, meandering conversations taught me something: The most important things that people need to tell you or hear from you often aren't the things they actually start to talk about, or even talk about at all. Niamh initially called about the breakup, but what she really needed was to feel heard, understood, and validated. The breakup was just the entry point.

Despite his complaints about the phone bill, my father understood this instinctively. When a local woman flagged him down on the main street to complain about the noise from the pub, he didn't just take notes and move on. He stood there for twenty minutes, listening to her concerns about the noise, yes, but also about her arthritis, worries about her son in London, and fears about getting older.

By the time he walked away, he'd learned that the noise wasn't really the problem–loneliness was. The pub noise was just keeping her awake at night, giving her too much time to think about everything she was worried about. His solution wasn't to shut down the pub; it was to organise a weekly bingo game for the local widows, so she had something to look forward to and people to talk to.

That's the kind of problem-solving that only happens when you listen out for what people *mean*, not just what they say.

My mum was also a master at this. In the hospital, she'd have patients who came in with one complaint but clearly needed something else entirely. The older man complaining about his medication schedule needed someone to explain his diagnosis in terms he could understand. The young mother worried about her child's breathing really needed reassurance that she was doing a good job.

Mum could have addressed the surface issue and moved on–and by hospital efficiency standards, she should have. But she understood that healing often happens in the spaces between official interactions. Like in the two minutes she spent explaining things in plain English. In the way she found a connection based on where they were from in Donegal or a distant cousin. In her ability to notice when someone was scared and needed extra reassurance. She wasn't just treating symptoms but treating people, and that meant listening.

This is where I learned that the most valuable skill in any relationship–personal or professional–is the ability to listen out for what isn't being said. To read the signals that tell you what someone really needs, even when they don't have the words for it themselves. To read between the lines.

And when you understand that, you see it everywhere. The best teachers weren't just the ones who knew their stuff inside and out; they were the ones who could tell when a student was struggling with something beyond the subject. The best shopkeepers weren't just efficient at the till; they were the ones who remembered which biscuits you liked, asked about your family, and knew exactly what you needed even when you weren't sure yourself.

I discovered the same thing in my teens, when I worked in bars and nightclubs. If you want to learn about people, those are the places to be.

I spent three years in the cloakroom and supper service at Schooner's nightclub and the Ark bar in Sligo. It was like getting a master's degree in human behaviour. A pub is where people go when they're celebrating, commiserating, or trying to escape whatever's happening in their lives. You learn quickly that half the job is serving people, and the other half is well … reading the room.

You'd have the lads who'd come in after a bad day at work, looking for someone to listen to their complaints. The couple having a quiet argument in the corner who needed space, not attention. The regular, who always ordered the same thing but whose mood you could read by how he asked for it. The tourists who were excited to be in Ireland but needed someone to make them feel welcome rather than just served.

The skill was knowing what each person needed and adapting accordingly. Sometimes that meant being chatty and friendly, other times efficient and invisible. It meant knowing when to cut someone off before they made a fool of themselves, and how to do it in a way that preserved their dignity. It meant using humour to defuse almost any situation but knowing that it had to be the right kind of humour at the right moment.

The difference between a good night and a bad night often came down to whether people felt seen and acknowledged, not just served drinks. People would tell you their life story if you showed genuine interest, but they'd clam up completely if they sensed you were just being polite.

Most importantly, I saw how the skills I was developing in life–reading people, adapting to their needs, and finding ways to connect–had real value in the world. This value was recognised when I landed my first job in advertising, in 2003.

During my college days in Ballyfermot, we had been forced to do group assignments. We were placed in a group with four other students for the year, and we'd have a month to complete each project. Most groups would work on it in the final week, cobbling something together that met the minimum requirements. But I'd start working on the project immediately, turn in my portion two weeks early, and spend the rest of the time helping my teammates with their parts. Not because I was particularly ambitious, but because I'd learned at the round table that people expected very little of me, and when I exceeded people's expectations, good things tended to happen.

After graduation, one of my group mates, Lesley, was working at a small advertising agency in Dublin. We had remained friends (still are to this day), and she remembered my work ethic and teamwork skills from the assignments. When she was asked to recommend someone for a different agency, she told her boss, "There's this girl from my college who actually cares about doing good work. She always turned up, did the work, and helped the rest of us with ours."

That recommendation got me an interview, and the interview landed me the job of account manager. Not because I was the smartest person they'd talked to but because I'd demonstrated something that apparently wasn't common: reliability, teamwork, and genuine care for the outcome. That aside, I had absolutely no experience, and it's fair to say I had no idea what I was doing.

The agency was small, scrappy, and handled a lot of what the big agencies didn't want: difficult clients, tight budgets, and impossible deadlines. I found myself gravitating toward the most challenging accounts, the ones that had other account managers ripping their hair out.

There was the restaurant chain owner who'd call screaming about his ads not running, only to discover he'd forgotten to approve his media plan. The retail client who'd change her mind about campaigns three times a week, then wondered why her brand message wasn't consistent. The startup founder who thought every creative execution was either brilliant or complete *shite*, with no middle ground.

Any other account manager saw these clients as punishment assignments. I saw them as puzzles to be solved, and the solution was always the same: figure out what they really needed, not just what they were asking for.

The restaurant owner wasn't angry about the ads–he was terrified that his business was failing and he didn't know how to fix it. Once I understood that, I could help him feel in control of his marketing while gently keeping him organised.

The retail client wasn't indecisive–she was under enormous pressure from her board to show results and was second-guessing every decision. Once I figured that out, I could structure our conversations to help her feel confident about her choices.

The founder wasn't being difficult–he was passionate about his product and frustrated that the marketing wasn't capturing what made it special. Once I understood his vision, I could help him communicate it in ways that resonated with his customers.

In each case, the *difficult* behaviour was communicating something deeper. I didn't know I was doing it, but I'd learned to listen for what wasn't being said, so I could respond to what they needed rather than just what they were complaining about.

While other people were stressed about managing client relationships *properly*, I was trying to understand each person as an individual. While they were worried about following the standard procedures, I was focused on finding creative solutions to their unique problems. (I haven't got much better at following processes even today.)

At the round table, I'd learned that people are complicated and don't always fit into neat categories. And indeed, the most interesting ones are often those who don't conform to expectations. That's why I had no expectations about how clients were "supposed" to behave.

The irony is that my colleagues often saw this as some kind of natural talent, as if I'd been born with the ability to handle difficult people. But it wasn't talent–it was a skill developed through years of being underestimated and having to prove myself in unconventional ways... ways that everyone can learn.

# THE DISCONNECTION ZONE | 3

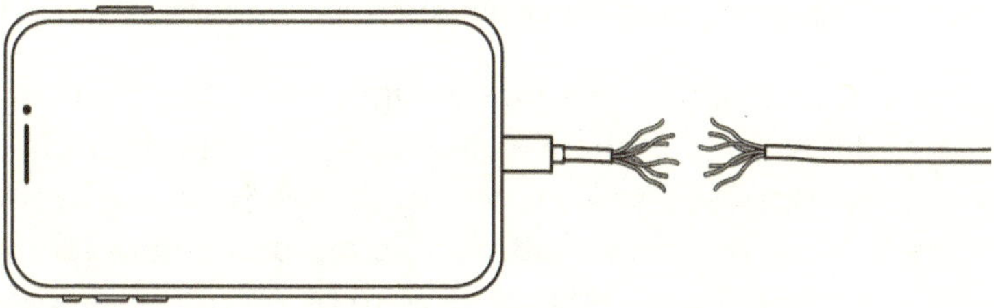

Something happened in the early 2000s that changed how we talk to each other, and I don't think we fully understood the consequences. I'm a child of the 80s, and life hadn't changed too much until the turn of the century, but then an acceleration happened. We got faster. Much faster. Email replaced phone calls, text messages replaced conversations, and suddenly we could communicate with dozens of people simultaneously while pretending to pay attention to the person sitting right in front of us.

It felt like progress. And in many ways, it was. But what we gained in speed and efficiency, we lost in depth and understanding.

I started noticing this shift around 2007. Everyone had smartphones; we'd rushed out to get them, and there was this palpable excitement about how much more connected we could be. We could stay in touch with friends constantly, share updates instantly, and never really be alone with our thoughts.

But something strange started happening. I was communicating with more people than ever before, yet I felt like I knew them less. My old friends from Sligo would send me quick texts about their lives–new jobs, relationships, weekend plans–but these bite-sized updates somehow felt less real than our old rambling phone calls that could stretch for hours.

One evening, sitting in a pub in Dublin with five friends, I realised that three of them were texting other people while we were supposed to be catching up. We were physically together but mentally scattered across a dozen different conversations. It wasn't that they were being rude–we were all doing it. It had become normal to be only *partially* present, constantly dividing our attention between the people in front of us and the people in our phones.

The real wake-up call came during the last few months of my father's life. In early 2009, he was diagnosed with a brain tumour. I found myself caught between wanting to be present with him and feeling compelled to keep everyone else updated on his condition. I'd send group texts to relatives, post careful updates on Facebook, and respond to the flood of concerned messages from friends.

But, no surprise, the most meaningful moments with my father happened when I put the phone away entirely. When I just sat with him, listening to his stories, holding his hand, being fully present in whatever time we had left.

I remember the day he got his final diagnosis. The doctor delivered the news with all the compassion he could muster, but my father's response surprised everyone in the room. Instead of falling apart or getting angry, he looked at the doctor and said, "Wow, your job is hard. I can't imagine having to give people bad news all day and the toll that takes on you."

The doctor was taken aback. With tears in his eyes, he thanked my father for his kindness and empathy. Even in his darkest moment, my father showed me the importance of human connection–of seeing the person in front of you, not just your own situation.

The weeks and months that followed taught me profound lessons about communication. Close friends and family struggled with how to respond. Some sent beautiful, heartfelt cards with handwritten notes. Others fired off quick texts: "Thinking of you 💕" or "Let me know if you need anything." Both were well-intentioned, but one felt like a real human connection to me and the other felt like checking a box.

After my father died, we had a three-day traditional Irish wake. For three days, we sat around Dad's body in the house, talking to him, talking about him, remembering him, singing, drinking, and eating. If you're unfamiliar with an Irish wake, you'd probably be horrified, but there's great healing during that time. People tell you stories you never knew about the person. You cry, laugh, and say goodbye. On the day of the funeral, I gave the eulogy, trying to squeeze as much of the man into it as possible–his humour, wisdom, and hopes for his children. There's never enough time.

After the funeral, I received dozens of messages of condolence through Facebook, texts, and emails. Each one meant something, but I found myself craving the friends who *actually* called. Who were willing to sit with the awkwardness of not knowing what to say to me. Who understood that my grief couldn't be properly addressed in 160 characters.

The difference wasn't in the sentiment, as I knew that everyone cared. The difference for me was in the effort they made, the time taken to be present with me rather than efficient. The people who showed up, who called, who sat with the discomfort of not having the perfect words, who understood that my grief required presence, not optimisation.

Years later, as I watched my mother struggle in a house filled with sad memories, I learned another lesson about long-term support. People are good at rallying around immediate crises, but grief doesn't follow a schedule. Every milestone–college degrees, new jobs, marriages, children–reminded us that he was no longer here. No matter how many years pass, when someone loses a parent, every day forward is a day further from the last time they saw them, heard their voice, felt their presence.

The experience also taught me about the enormous difference that empathy makes in professional relationships. When my employer texted two days after the funeral and opened his message with "When are you coming back to work?", that lack of understanding–the inability to see me as a whole human being going through the worst experience of my life–damaged our relationship permanently. My faith in him and the company ended that day.

I wasn't asking for much, and I don't expect my boss to turn up on my doorstep with flowers and a handwritten card. All it would have taken was to begin his text with "Hey, how are you doing?", leading with human connection rather than a cold, transactional exchange. I would have given the same answer either way, but the latter would have made me feel like a human.

Never underestimate the impact of empathy, or the lack of it. In our digital age, it's become easier than ever to treat people as resources to be managed rather than humans to be supported. But the companies and leaders who understand this–who take the time to see the whole person–earn loyalty that no efficiency system can replicate.

But perhaps the most important lesson came from my father himself, even in his final months. Despite everything he was facing, he never lost his ability to see and connect with other people. When he thanked the doctor for the difficulty of his job, when he made us sing happy birthday on what would be his last day out of bed, he was teaching me that human connection isn't something we do when life is easy–it's what we need most when life is hard.

His death taught me that some conversations can't be optimised, some relationships can't be managed efficiently, and some human experiences can't be rushed or multi-tasked. The people who understood this–who called instead of texting, who sat with the discomfort instead of rushing to fix things–were the relationships that deepened during that time.

This experience fundamentally changed how I think about communication and efficiency. I noticed this in my friendships too. I had friends I talked to constantly through messages and social media, but when we met in person, there were surprising gaps in what we really knew about each other's lives. We'd been sharing the highlights and the logistics, but missing the deeper currents–the doubts, dreams, and everyday struggles that make up the real texture of a human life.

This is what we're losing in our rush to communicate efficiently in the age of technology. We're becoming brilliant at exchanging information, but we're forgetting how to simply be with each other. We're optimised for response time instead of response quality, for convenience instead of connection. Carol and my "Mercy Girls" could waste hours talking about absolutely nothing–while Enda, Darren, Brian, Marc, David–taught me how to argue with, laugh with, and sit in silence with almost anything. None of us were efficient conversationalists, but we learned how to read each other in those moments.

The solution isn't to abandon technology–that's neither realistic nor desirable. But we need to become more intentional about how we use it. We need to recognise that different kinds of tools serve different purposes. Some things need to be fast and efficient. But other things need to be slow and personal.

Sometimes, we need to take a lesson from the 90s and pick up the phone! Instead of letting misunderstandings compound through digital miscommunication, we can shift to a medium that enables better connection and understanding. (We'll look at this more in chapter 7.)

But this is not about being anti-technology (after all, this is a book about AI, among other things). It's about being pro-human. It's about recognising that while digital tools can make us more efficient, they can't make us more understanding. And understanding–real, deep, human understanding–is what creates the trust, love, and connection that makes life meaningful.

When you're fully present with someone–not divided between them and your phone, not rushing towards the next task–you remember why you care about them in the first place. And they recognise that you care about them.

The choice is ours. We can continue down the path of hyper-efficiency, optimising our way out of the human connections that make life meaningful. Or we can learn to use our incredible tools to create more space for the slow, inefficient, gloriously human work of truly understanding one another.

# THE GREAT SEPARATION | 4

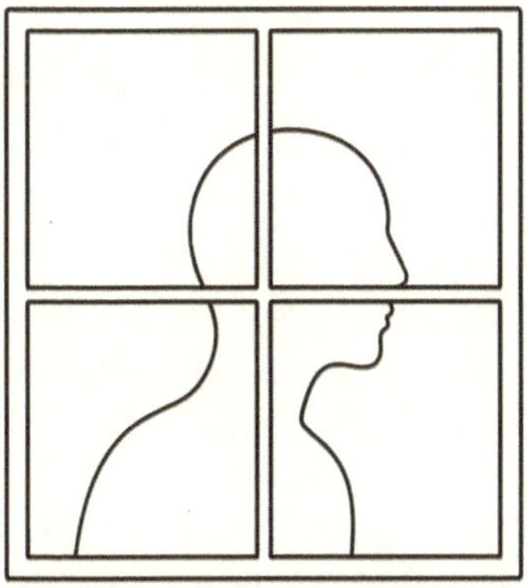

While I learned those lessons about disconnection back in 2009, the world learned those lessons collectively a decade later. COVID-19 was a global experiment in human connection that none of us signed up for. And it became the most profound lesson in what happens when systems fail us, and what saves us if they do.

I'll never forget those early family Zoom calls. My poor father-in-law, bless him, couldn't figure out the audio settings. Week after week, we could either see him gesticulating wildly or hear his muffled voice, but we could rarely do both. With two young kids at home and the chaos of sudden remote everything, those technical fumbles felt like a metaphor for how disconnected we'd all become overnight.

Every family had its version of this story. The grandmother who kept accidentally hanging up on everyone. The teenager who discovered virtual backgrounds and spent entire family dinners as a floating head in front of the Eiffel Tower. The uncle who never figured out he was on mute and spent months talking to himself. We laugh about it now, but at the time, it felt like we were losing something essential about being human together.

The day before lockdown, I had a Paint with Prosecco team outing in Dublin city centre. The atmosphere was eerie–everyone knew the country was shutting down the next day. We painted; we drank prosecco and tried to pretend it was just another team-building exercise. But there was something in the air, a collective understanding that this might be our last *normal* interaction for a while.

Walking home that evening, the streets were already ghostly quiet. Shops were posting hastily written "Closed until further notice" signs. The few people I passed moved with purpose, eyes down, already practicing the social distancing that would become second nature. That was it. The next morning, we were all working from bedrooms, kitchens, and whatever corner we could claim as "office space".

I genuinely thought I might shrivel up and die during COVID. I'm a social creature, and the sudden disconnection felt existential. The first few weeks were genuinely difficult. I found myself talking to just about everyone for longer than necessary, just desperate for human interaction beyond my immediate family. But something interesting happened instead of the social withering I expected.

I discovered that the first five minutes of every Zoom call–the time we previously used to spend on small talk while people grabbed coffee or found seats–could be used to build deeper relationships than I'd ever had in traditional office environments.

Instead of rushing into business, I started every call the same way: "How are you really doing? How's your family coping with all this?"

And people opened up in ways they never had before. In physical meetings, there are so many distractions. People are checking their phones, thinking about their next meeting, watching who's walking by in the corridor. But on Zoom, especially in those early days when everyone was still figuring it out, there was an intimacy to seeing inside someone's home, meeting their kids or pets, witnessing their authentic environment.

On one call with a particularly stern colleague, who had always been all business, never one for casual conversation, her toddler wandered into frame wearing nothing but a diaper and a tiara. She was mortified, but I said, "That's exactly the kind of interruption we need right now." We spent ten minutes talking about how she was managing work and parenting, and our professional relationship was forever changed for the better.

This became a pattern. The vulnerability of everyone's situation created permission for genuine conversations. People shared their fears, their coping strategies, their discoveries about themselves and their families. The formal barriers that typically separate professional relationships started to dissolve.

My network expanded, which surprised everyone who knew how much I thrived on face-to-face interaction. I started scheduling calls with international colleagues I'd never made time for before. Without the constraint of geographic proximity, everyone became equally accessible. A team member in Singapore was just as easy to connect with as someone who used to sit three desks away.

These weren't networking calls in the traditional sense. They were human check-ins that happened to be between people who also worked together. Twenty minutes of genuine conversation about how someone was handling isolation, what new interests they'd discovered, what they were struggling with. Then ten minutes of efficient business discussion. The ratio mattered. The personal connection made the professional collaboration more effective, not less.

But COVID had more lessons to teach me about human connection than I could have imagined. The biggest one came in the most unlikely place–a hospital ward, separated from my newborn daughter, learning that sometimes our deepest need for connection emerges precisely when we're most isolated.

When Willow arrived via C-section, my wife Geraldine held our daughter for the first time wearing a surgical mask, her smile hidden but her eyes shining with tears of relief and love. But birth, even during a pandemic, is messy and unpredictable. During the delivery, complications meant my lungs began filling with fluid–though we wouldn't understand this for days.

Six days after bringing Willow home, I found myself gasping for air every time I tried to lie down. The sensation was terrifying–like drowning while surrounded by air. My wife, exhausted from sleepless nights and the overwhelming adjustment to life with three kids, initially thought I was having anxiety attacks. "You're panicking," she said gently, bouncing our crying daughter while watching me struggle to breathe. "It's just the stress of everything." And how could I blame her for thinking that? The world had gone mad. We were all panicking about something.

But deep in my chest, I felt something wrong, something physical and urgent that had nothing to do with my mental state. When I lay down, fluid seemed to shift and settle, pressing against my lungs like invisible hands squeezing the air out of me. I'd sit up gasping, heart racing, desperate for the simple act of drawing breath that I'd taken for granted for many years.

This was during the height of COVID hysteria, when every cough sent people scrambling, when every respiratory symptom carried the weight of a potential death sentence. I went to the maternity hospital first, where a harried doctor barely looked up from his clipboard. "Everything's fine," he said dismissively. "It's anxiety. Very common."

But mothers know their bodies. I knew this wasn't anxiety. This was my body failing me when I needed it most–when I had a six-day-old daughter who depended on me completely.

Eventually, desperation drove me to ring the D-Doc service, a 24-hour emergency line. The nurse who answered didn't just hear my symptoms–she heard my fear, confusion, and my maternal desperation bleeding through the phone line.

"Tell me exactly what's happening when you try to lie down," she said, and something in her voice made me stop trying to sound calm and rational.

"I feel like I'm drowning," I whispered, afraid that saying it out loud would make it more real. "Like there's water in my chest and it's going to fill up my mouth and nose."

The silence stretched for several seconds. Then she said, "Get to a hospital immediately. Don't drive yourself. Call an ambulance if you need to." Then my Irishness kicked in, and I said, "It's okay, I'll get a taxi; the drama of an ambulance is not for me."

But the urgency in her voice sent ice through my veins. This wasn't anxiety or post-birth hysteria. This was real and dangerous.

So, there I was, six days postpartum, milk coming in and making my breasts ache, having to choose between staying with my newborn daughter and potentially saving my own life. The primal pull toward Willow was overwhelming–every cell in my body screamed at me not to leave her, not to break the invisible cord that still connected us even though the physical one had been cut.

I stood in our bedroom with shaking hands, looking at her tiny sleeping face. She was so small, so dependent, so perfectly formed. What if something happened to me? What if I never came home? What if these were our last moments together?

My wife tried to be strong, but I could see the fear in her eyes too. "Go," she said firmly. "We'll be here when you get back." But neither of us knew if that was true.

Because I couldn't breathe, the hospital immediately assumed I had COVID and whisked me away to the isolation ward. The irony was brutal–I'd spent six days bonding with my daughter, only to be separated from her by the very safety measures designed to protect families like ours.

They tested me–negative, thankfully, but then blood tests revealed something potentially worse: suspected blood clots. The news hit like a physical blow, punching the air from my already struggling lungs. Six days after having a baby, with hormones still flooding my system like emotional tidal waves and now facing a potentially life-threatening condition that could leave my kids without me.

The COVID protocols were ruthlessly efficient. Mask on, temperature checked, forms filled, bed assigned. I was processed through the system like a package being sorted–necessary, systematic, but utterly devoid of human warmth.

They brought me to the emergency room and left me on a gurney in a corridor that smelled of disinfectant and fear. Patients groaned behind curtains. Machines beeped their electronic warnings. Staff moved with practiced efficiency; all eyes focused on charts rather than faces.

I started to cry behind my mask–not just from pain or fear, but from the overwhelming loneliness of being reduced to a case number when what I needed most was human connection, someone to see me as a person rather than a problem to be solved.

That's when the nurses noticed–not my medical condition, but my human one. They saw a woman crying alone on a trolley and made a choice that had nothing to do with efficiency or protocols. They brought me into a small side room, away from the chaos, giving me privacy for my breakdown.

One of them told the tea lady about my situation. She had been making her rounds with mechanical precision, offering standard tea and toast with the enthusiasm of someone who'd done this exact job thousands of times before. She was probably in her sixties, grey hair pulled back practically, deep Dublin accent from the inner city, a voice like she smoked fifty cigarettes a day, wearing comfortable shoes that had walked these corridors for years. When I first saw her, she seemed like part of the hospital machinery–efficient, functional, unremarkable.

But the moment she heard that I'd just given birth six days ago, everything about her changed. Her entire posture shifted. Her eyes went from distant to laser-focused on my face. She set down her tea trolley and really looked at me–not as a patient to be served, but as a mother who was scared and alone.

"Oh, love," she said, and those two words contained more warmth than all the medical consultations combined. "Oh, you poor thing." She disappeared and returned minutes later with a proper pot of tea–not the standard hospital brew, but something she'd made specially, strong and steaming. She arranged a plate of buttered toast, cutting it into neat triangles like you might do for a child.

"You need to eat," she said firmly. "You need your strength. Everything's going to be okay, and you're going to be reunited with your baby soon."

But she didn't stop there. She pulled up a chair–sat down beside my trolley–and stayed with me while I cried. She told me about her own children, born decades earlier, and how terrifying those early days had been even without a global pandemic complicating everything.

"I remember thinking I was going to break my first one just by holding her wrong," she said, laughing softly. "Convinced myself I was the worst mother in the world every time she cried. But look–she's forty now, has three babies of her own, and she still calls me every Sunday."

Her stories weren't profound or life-changing. They were ordinary, human, real. And they were exactly what I needed–proof that other women had survived the overwhelming responsibility of motherhood, that this terror and love and confusion were part of the universal human experience of being a mother.

This woman had no medical training relevant to my condition. She couldn't diagnose my breathing problems or prescribe treatment. But she understood something, like my mother, that the medical system had missed: Healing isn't just about fixing what's broken in our bodies–it's about remembering what connects us to each other (although this sentence structure is now used, or some may say overused, by AI, it was my granny who used to say this line. She's been quoted in various medical books, so maybe AI learned it from her!).

When the doctor came to tell me that I needed a CT scan, my carefully constructed composure crumbled completely. It was a bank holiday weekend, appointments were full, and I wasn't considered urgent enough to jump the queue. They couldn't treat my symptoms until they knew what was causing them, but I'd have to wait days for answers staying in the hospital.

"I can't wait," I said, the words coming out as a desperate whisper. "I have to get back to my baby and kids."

The pull was beyond rational thought, beyond medical necessity. It was primal, cellular, the same force that makes mothers lift cars off trapped children or run into burning buildings. Every moment away from Willow felt like abandonment, like I was failing at the most basic requirement of motherhood: being there.

The medical team exchanged glances–the look healthcare workers give each other when dealing with an *irrational* patient who doesn't understand the system's constraints.

But one nurse–a woman probably my own age, with kind eyes above her mask–looked at me differently. She saw the desperation, the maternal panic, the way I was literally vibrating with the need to return to my baby. "Let me see what I can do," she said quietly.

Twenty minutes later, she was back. She'd walked up to the CT radiology ward–not called, walked–and found the radiologist on duty. A woman from Monaghan, who was also a mother.

"I told her about you," the nurse explained. "About how you just had a baby six days ago, how distressed you are, how you'll leave without treatment if we don't get answers tonight."

The radiologist had agreed to stay past her shift, to squeeze me in between emergency cases, to do whatever it took to get me the scan I needed so I could return to my kids.

The walk to radiology felt like a pilgrimage through fluorescent-lit corridors that all looked the same. My body still felt broken from the C-section–every step a reminder of what I'd been through, every movement a negotiation between my desperate need to move forward and my body's insistence that it wasn't ready.

The radiologist was waiting when I arrived, and I could see immediately that she was tired–the kind of bone-deep exhaustion that comes from long shifts and emotional labour. She could have processed me efficiently, got the job done, and gone home to her family.

Instead, she looked me in the eye and said, "I heard you just had a baby. This must be terrifying."

"I keep thinking about Willow and the boys," I whispered, tears streaming down my face again. "What if they need me and I'm not there? What if something happens to me and they grow up without ever really knowing me?"

The radiologist nodded. "I have three children too," she said simply. "The youngest is six months old. I understand."

Getting me into the CT scanner was a logistics challenge–I was essentially cut in half from the C-section, unable to move normally, and every position sent shooting pains through my abdomen. She took her time, adjusting the table, finding angles that wouldn't cause additional damage, talking me through each step with a gentleness that went far beyond professional competence. "This is going to be loud," she warned, her hand briefly touching my shoulder. "But I'll be right here watching, and we'll have answers soon."

As the machine hummed and clicked around me, I thought about the choice she'd made. She could have gone home to her own six-month-old, could have left my case for the next shift. Instead, she'd seen another mother in crisis and chosen to help, understanding that sometimes medical care means more than just diagnostic procedures–it means one human being refusing to let another human being suffer alone.

Back in the emergency ward, the results brought both relief and new terror. No blood clots–my lungs were simply filled with fluid. But that meant admission to the hospital, potentially for days.

"I can't be admitted," I said, panic making my voice high and thin. "I'll go to my local doctor. They can manage this as an outpatient."

The medical team looked at me with a mixture of professional concern and human understanding. They knew I was making an irrational decision, but they also knew the pull I was feeling.

"It's not safe," one doctor said gently. "Your oxygen levels are dangerously low. We need to monitor you, drain the fluid, and make sure there aren't other complications."

But the primitive part of my brain wasn't listening to medical logic. It was screaming at me to return to my baby. "I'll come back if it gets worse," I promised, knowing even as I said it that this was probably a lie I was telling myself.

They let me leave. I made it exactly four hours at home. Four hours of holding Willow, breathing in her perfect baby smell, feeling her tiny fingers curl around mine. Four hours of pretending everything was normal, that I was able to will my body back to health through sheer maternal determination.

But as evening became night, the fluid in my lungs seemed to settle and expand. I found myself sitting upright in bed, unable to lie down at all, gasping for air. My wife found me there at 2am, eyes wide with fear, lips slightly blue from lack of oxygen.

"We're going back," she said, no longer willing to humour my denial.

I packed a small overnight bag as if I were preparing for battle, trying to choose which personal items might comfort me during whatever came next. I stood over Willow for what felt like hours but was probably only minutes, memorising her sleeping face, the way her tiny chest rose and fell with each perfect breath.

"I'll be back," I whispered to her, though I wasn't sure I believed it. "Mammy will be back soon."

This time, when I walked through the hospital doors, something was different. The same staff who had processed me earlier that day now greeted me with recognition and concern that felt genuinely human.

"You came back," the admitting nurse said, and there was relief in her voice. "We were worried about you."

They'd been worried about me. Not just about my medical case or their liability, but about me as a person who had walked out against medical advice because she couldn't bear to be separated from her newborn daughter.

They found me a bed on a stroke ward–the only space available during COVID restrictions. The stroke ward was a strange place to learn about human connection. Patients surrounded by machines that measured heartbeats and brain activity, many unable to communicate normally, all of us cut off from family visits by COVID protocols.

Without family visitors to rely on, patients and staff had to go the extra mile for each other. The nurses and care staff asked if I needed a hug, and yes, it broke the rules, but it felt like my heart was breaking and they knew it. And they all rallied around me–the young mother who shouldn't have been there, who was leaking breast milk and crying about her baby at unpredictable intervals.

For three days, they ran tests and offered theories. Heart failure. Kidney problems. Rare complications from childbirth. Each possibility felt like a door slamming shut on the life I'd imagined–the healthy, energetic mother I'd planned to be. At this point, my limbs had started to swell too.

The cardiologist was young and serious, delivering his initial assessment with the gravity of someone announcing a death sentence: "We think it's your heart. This is likely permanent. You'll need to completely change your lifestyle, limit physical activity, and possibly need medication for the rest of your life."

It took a pulmonologist (a lung specialist) to finally piece together what had happened. He reviewed my birth records, examined the timeline of my symptoms, and asked questions no one else had thought to ask.

"Tell me about the delivery," he said. "How much fluid did you receive? Were there complications with the IV?"

As he talked through the possibilities, the real story emerged. During the complicated delivery, I'd received large amounts of IV fluids. And apparently, my body is unusually absorbent–instead of processing these fluids normally, I'd absorbed them directly into my lung tissue.

"You're like a sponge," he explained with a slight smile. "Most people would have processed and eliminated these fluids within hours. Your body held on to them."

Not heart failure. Not a life-threatening condition. Not a permanent condition. Just a quirk of biology had turned a routine medical intervention into a frightening crisis, with a simple solution: take diuretics for 4 hours to clear my lungs and body.

The relief was so overwhelming I started laughing and crying simultaneously. "You're going home to your baby," he said.

The months that followed taught me that crisis doesn't create character–it reveals it. Some organisations, like some individuals, retreated into rigid self-protection when faced with uncertainty. They implemented monitoring systems, eliminated *unnecessary* interactions, and focused purely on measurable outputs.

Others became paralysed by the complexity of caring for everyone's emotional needs while still accomplishing essential work.

But the most resilient organisations, like the healthcare system that had cared for me, found ways to be systematically competent while remaining genuinely human. They used technology to enhance rather than replace human connection. They created efficiency not by eliminating empathy, but by making empathy more intentional and effective.

I thought about the tea lady, who could have simply served standard tea and moved on, but chose to sit with a scared mother and share stories that provided exactly the comfort I needed in that moment.

I thought about the radiologist who stayed late, not because efficiency demanded it, but because she understood what another mother was experiencing and chose to help.

I thought about the community of patients and staff who created connection and care even when systems were designed to keep us apart. These weren't accidents. These were choices–individual decisions to prioritise human understanding alongside professional competence.

Back home, recovering and adapting to life with three kids during lockdown, another unexpected connection emerged. My wife and I finally had time to work on our garden, and suddenly we were talking to neighbours we'd barely acknowledged before.

It started over the wall: socially distanced conversations while we were all outside more than usual. Our kids had a water balloon fight with the neighbours' children, lobbing balloons over the fence because they couldn't play in the same space. They were laughing and shrieking with joy, separated by a physical barrier but completely connected in the moment.

This became a metaphor for everything I was learning. Physical separation didn't have to mean emotional disconnection. Barriers could become bridges when people chose to see them that way.

The children led the way, as they often do. They didn't see the wall as a barrier–they saw it as an interesting challenge to overcome. They passed drawings back and forth, played games that worked across physical separation, and created elaborate treasure hunts that spanned multiple properties.

Watching them reminded me of something I'd learned in that hospital ward: Connection isn't about proximity or convenience.

It's about creativity, intentionality, and the willingness to find new ways to reach each other when the old ways don't work. Even when we can't be there in person.

That experience–giving birth during a pandemic, being hospitalised and separated from my newborn, depending on the kindness of strangers in a system designed around protocols rather than people–fundamentally changed how I understand the relationship between individual humans and the systems we create.

We are instinctively driven toward connection, towards relating to each other. It's encoded in our DNA, expressed in everything from a mother's desperate need to return to her baby to a tea lady's impulse to comfort a stranger with stories and kindness to children having water balloon fights over a wall.

# THE SCIENCE OF HUMAN CONNECTION | 5

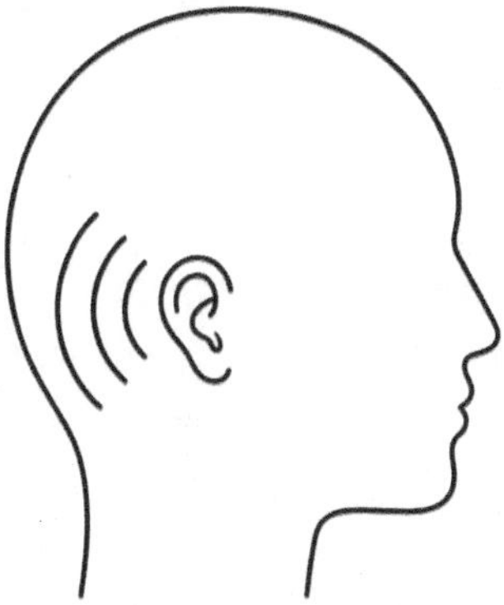

When I was eight years old, I was sitting in the front room of an older neighbour's house in Leitrim while my parents made what was supposed to be a quick welfare check. She was 83, lived alone since her husband had passed, and by all official metrics, she was managing fine. But within minutes of walking into her house, my parents knew something the data couldn't capture.

They saw it in the way her face transformed when we knocked–from wary suspicion to pure joy. They noticed how she kept refilling the teapot, offering more biscuits, asking just one more question about anything at all. They recognised the subtle choreography of loneliness: the way she lingered in doorways, the reluctance to say goodbye, the brightening that came simply from having voices in her sitting room.

My parents had a choice: follow protocol and move on or follow their gut and respond to what they were seeing. They chose to stay. Two hours later, her entire demeanor had changed. She stood straighter, smiled more genuinely, and had that glow that comes from feeling truly seen and valued.

That afternoon taught me the most important information isn't always spoken, but in the pauses, the energy, the things people don't say, the way they position themselves, and the subtle signals that tell you what they really need.

I'm not a science girl, and I won't pretend to be one. But I do know that human brains evolved over millions of years to navigate social relationships and require human connection like this. We have specialised neural networks for reading facial expressions, interpreting vocal tones, and understanding the subtle cues that tell us whether someone is trustworthy, interested, or potentially threatening.

Before having kids almost killed me, I worked at another Dublin advertising agency in my late twenties. My company saw the value of understanding the science of humans and trained us in neurolinguistics to better understand our clients and maybe more effectively access their budgets. It was very forward-thinking for a Dublin-based agency at the time, but I benefit from that investment nearly every day.

What fascinated me during that training was realising the skills I'd started developing at the round table–reading the teacher's moods, understanding what my classmates really needed, adapting my approach to different personalities–weren't just random talents. They were based on actual brain science.

When we interact with someone face to face, like my parents and my neighbour, these ancient systems are working at full capacity. We're processing dozens of micro-signals simultaneously:

*body language, eye contact, vocal inflection, timing, energy level*. Most of this processing happens unconsciously, but it creates a rich understanding of the other person's emotional state and intentions. The better we are at this, the more we understand people.

This is why my sister Nat has been so successful as a teacher at Mercy College in Sligo, the same secondary school I attended. She's been there for over 25 years, and what strikes me most when we're out is how often kids come up to us. They always start with, "Are you Ms. McDevitt's sister? You look just like her." But what they really want to tell us is how she changed their lives.

There was the girl who struggled with dyslexia like me, convinced she was stupid until Nat saw something in her face during class–that look of understanding followed by frustration when she couldn't get the words out. She recognised the same signals I'd shown at the round table. She didn't just give her extra help with reading but helped her discover she was brilliant at understanding people and solving problems creatively. Now, that girl runs her own business.

There was the girl from a chaotic home situation who came to school each morning with the kind of tiredness that comes from stress, not just lack of sleep. Nat could read it in her posture, her reluctance to make eye contact, the way she sat slightly apart from other students. Instead of just focusing on academic performance, Nat started checking in with her every morning–not about schoolwork, but about how she was really doing.

"Ms. McDevitt was the first adult who seemed to actually see me," the girl told us years later in a local bar she was working weekends in. "She could tell when I was having a rough time at home just by looking at me. She made me feel like I mattered."

These days, digital communication strips away most of these signals. When we interact through screens, keyboards, and speakers, we're operating with a fraction of the social information our brains are designed to process in person. The challenge is the same as always: understanding what people really need, but the tools we use today are completely different and those signals can be harder to spot.

I learned this the hard way during a cross-functional project kick-off call. I was in my home office in Dublin, on a video call with a team spread across three time zones. The meeting was going well by all traditional metrics–we were covering the agenda, everyone was participating, and the technical details were being sorted out. But something felt off with a stakeholder. She was saying all the right things, but there was something in her tone, a hesitancy in her responses, that made me think she wasn't fully on board.

In a face-to-face meeting, I would have trusted that instinct and found a way to check in with her. But on the video call, with six other people present and a packed agenda, I let it slide. We finished the meeting on time, everyone seemed satisfied, and I moved on to the next item on my calendar.

Two weeks later, the project hit a major snag. My colleague had concerns about the approach we'd agreed on, but she hadn't felt comfortable raising them in the group call. The hesitancy I'd noticed wasn't uncertainty about the technical details–it was her being unsure about whether she could trust us to listen to her concerns.

By the time we had a proper one-on-one conversation, the project was behind schedule, and my colleague was frustrated.

"I tried to signal that I had concerns," she told me, "but everyone seemed so eager to move forward, and I didn't want to be the one to slow things down."

That conversation taught me something crucial: The signals are still there in digital communication, but they're often more subtle. They disappear quickly if you're not paying attention. My colleague had been trying to communicate her concerns, but not through her words–through her tone, energy, and body language on the video call.

After that call, I started paying more attention to these digital signals, or *digital body language*, and it changed everything. I noticed the difference between someone's enthusiasm for a project being genuine versus when they were just being compliant. I could tell when a colleague was happy versus when they were satisfied but not excited. I learned to recognise when someone was struggling with something beyond what they had explicitly asked for help with. It's possible, but you need to know what to look for.

And that's what's interesting: The people who excel at digital communication have learned to compensate for the limitations of screens and keyboards. They use techniques that artificially recreate some of the social signals that we'd normally pick up on in person.

My father understood these techniques instinctively, even though he worked in an era before video calls and instant messaging. When he couldn't read someone's face during a phone conversation with another Garda station, he'd pay extra attention to vocal tones, the pace of speech, to what wasn't being said. He'd ask more direct questions: "You sound tired, rough day?" or, "I can hear something in your voice, what's really going on?"

The partners I work with who are most successful at building relationships across digital channels have learned similar techniques. They're more explicit about their emotional states in emails: "I'm excited about this opportunity, but I'm also nervous about the timeline." They check for understanding more frequently in video calls: "Does this approach make sense to you? I can't read your expression."

But most importantly, the best communicators know when to abandon the computer entirely and shift to phone calls or in-person meetings. They recognise that some types of interaction require a different type of human communication. (In chapter 7, we'll look at which tools are best for which job.)

During the COVID lockdowns when Nat had to teach remotely, she could deliver the curriculum through video calls, but she couldn't read her students' faces clearly enough to know who was struggling emotionally. So, she started scheduling individual phone calls with each student–not about coursework, just to check in as humans.

"I needed to hear their voices properly," she told me. "You can tell so much from how someone says, 'I'm fine' that you can't pick up through a computer screen."

Nat was picking up on something important, something that might seem contradictory. It's tempting to assume that we get more communication signals through a video call because we can see *and* hear the other person on our screen. But here's the thing: Science tells us that voice calls rather than video calls can lead to more engaged and deeper conversations as the voice conveys a wealth of information through tone and "paralinguistics".

Voice-only conversations require less mental energy than video calls as we're not having to process complex visual information.

They're also less intrusive because we are not on camera, and this enables us to focus on the conversation without worrying about how we look, our surroundings, or the room's lighting. They avoid issues like poor video quality, lagging, and frozen screens, which can disrupt the flow of conversation, make it harder to gauge reactions, result in talking over each other, or be a distraction.

As I've said before (and will no doubt say again), the solution isn't to abandon digital communication entirely–it's to be more intentional about developing our human connection skills and recognise when tech helps that and when it hinders it. This means creating opportunities for real conversation, even if it's not the most efficient option. It means practicing the same attention to human signals that my father used in his community work, that Nat uses in her classroom, and that I learned at the round table. It's the skills of connection.

# THE SKILLS OF HUMAN CONNECTION | 6

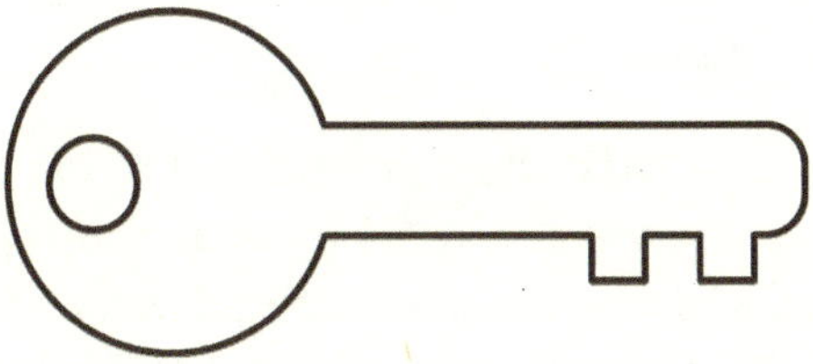

Early on in life, I learned that every "difficult" person has a story that explains their behaviour. The key is being curious enough to find that story and patient enough to respond to it appropriately, just like back at the first advertising agency, where I enjoyed working with the "difficult" clients.

That skill, being able to "de-escalate" people, has served me well throughout my career, and it continues to serve me now. But what fascinates me is how few people recognise it as a skill at all. Like at the first agency I worked at, they saw it as either natural talent (which it isn't) or as something that can't be developed (which it can).

The truth is that reading people, building rapport, and managing complex relationships are skills like any other. They require practice, attention, and the willingness to learn from mistakes, which are admittedly not that easy. They are also the skills that our education system largely ignores, and that some workplaces actively discourage in favour of more *measurable* competencies.

This is a mistake, frankly. In a world where technology can handle more of the routine tasks that used to require human attention, the skills of being able to understand people, build trust, and navigate complex social dynamics become increasingly valuable.

The round table kids often developed these skills out of necessity. We learned to read rooms, adapt to different personalities, and find ways to connect because we had to. We learned that surprising people in positive ways opened doors that credentials and connections alone could not. And for some reason I can't explain (no pun about table shapes), we saw things in a full-circle way.

However, these skills shouldn't be the exclusive domain of the misfits and the underestimated. They should be recognised, valued, and systematically developed. In a world that's becoming increasingly automated, the ability to create genuine human connection isn't just a nice-to-have anymore–it's become essential.

This is something I think about a lot in my current role. I work with companies that are brilliant at the technical aspects of marketing and sales but sometimes struggle with the human elements. They can build sophisticated campaigns and analyse complex data, but they have trouble reading client moods, adapting their communication style, or navigating the interpersonal dynamics that make partnerships successful.

The solution obviously isn't to abandon technology or somehow become "a people person" overnight. The solution is to recognise that relationship skills are learnable, valuable, and complementary to technical expertise. Just as we invest in learning new software or staying current with industry trends, we should invest in developing our ability to understand and connect with people.

Because at the end of the day, business *is* about people. Technology can make us more efficient, but it can't replace the fundamentally human skills of building trust, creating understanding, and making people feel valued. That work requires skills that can be learned, but only if we recognise their importance and make the effort to develop them.

I learned this lesson in business from my darling aunt and uncle, Tina and William. They taught me many things as a kid, like how to be a decent human being, and the importance of family and laughter. A lot of laughter. Tina had a special way of connecting with others, often with her laugh alone.

William still runs a haulage company called Duffy Express in Donegal. He is brilliant at this, although he would likely think everyone is. When a customer calls to book a delivery, he'll ask questions that seem to have nothing to do with transport: "How urgent was this, really? What was the delivery for? Who was waiting for it? Was this part of a bigger opportunity?" Most of his competitors would see these questions as unnecessary small talk, but William understands that behind every transport request is a human story. And understanding that story is what separates good service from exceptional service.

This level of understanding made him a great employer and businessman. Once, a customer needed a rush delivery to Cork. On the surface, it was straightforward: pickup in Dublin, delivery by end of day, higher fee for the urgent service. But

William's questions revealed that this was for a wedding, and the delivery was a dress that had been held up by another supplier, and the bride was already stressed about everything else going wrong.

Instead of just arranging the transport, William called the shop in Cork to make sure they'd be there to receive it, checked in with the customer twice during the day to confirm progress, and even waited to make sure the dress fit properly before leaving. It wasn't in his job description but it was the difference between a satisfied customer and a customer for life.

That bride's family used William's company for the next twenty years and recommended him to dozens of other people. The extra hour he spent on that delivery paid for itself hundreds of times over, but only because he understood he wasn't just in the transport business–he was in the peace-of-mind business. Or maybe he's a hopeless romantic.

On my own wedding day, William asked if he and Tina could drive me to my wedding. He was just recovering from throat cancer, but he asked because he said he wanted to return a favour to my dad, who had passed away and had driven him to his wedding. Now maybe it was, but I will always feel that they wanted to support me on that day because they knew I would be missing my dad. Him and Tina knew, in that moment, it was the support I needed.

This is what I mean when I talk about "reading the room". It's not just about understanding the immediate social dynamics; it's about understanding the deeper currents that drive human behaviour. What people are really worried about, what they're hoping for, what they need to feel supported.

Unfortunately, these skills are becoming rarer. We're so focused on efficiency, getting through our to-do lists, managing our digital communications, that we're losing the ability to slow down and really see the people in front of us. I notice this in meetings where everyone is half-listening while managing their other priorities, like checking their emails. I see it in customer service interactions that address the technical issue but miss the emotional context entirely, like why the person is upset about something in the first place. I see it in relationships where people are so busy optimising their connections and finding their LinkedIn QR that they forget to truly connect.

The irony is that these skills have never been more valuable! In a world where most interactions are becoming transactional, the ability to create genuine human connection stands out more than ever. The companies that understand this, that invest in people who can read between the lines and respond to what customers need, are the ones that build lasting loyalty, like William's business.

And as we saw in previous chapters, it's not just about business. These skills make everything better. Friendships become deeper when you put your phone away and genuinely listen to them over a coffee, understand their story, and make them feel seen. Marriages become stronger when you understand that "How was your day?" is often really asking, "Do you see me? Do you care about what I'm going through?" Parenting becomes more effective when you realise that a child's bad behaviour is usually telling you something else entirely: They're tired, overwhelmed, worried, or need more connection with you.

Even dealing with bureaucracy becomes easier when you understand that the person behind the desk is probably dealing with difficult people all day and will respond much better to someone who treats them like a human being rather than an obstacle. You see their story, and they see yours.

I learned this lesson when I was trying to sort out a problem with my driving licence. I'd been to the driver's licence office three times in Clarehall, each time getting more frustrated with the lady who kept telling me I needed different documents. On the fourth visit, instead of launching into my complaint, I asked how her day was going.

"Brutal," she said. "I've had people shouting at me all morning about things that aren't my fault."

So I said, "That sounds exhausting. I really appreciate you taking the time to help me figure this out."

Her entire demeanor changed. She spent ten minutes walking me through exactly what I needed, even calling another department to confirm the requirements, and sorting my issue within the week. Same person, same problem, completely different outcome–just because I took thirty seconds to acknowledge her as a human being.

My grandmother used to say, "Everyone you meet is fighting a battle you know nothing about." She was right, of course, but I'll add this: Everyone you meet is hoping for something that you might be able to provide. Not necessarily material things, but recognition, understanding, respect, or the feeling that they matter. Even if it takes a bit longer.

This is, essentially, the thing we're losing: the skill of slowing down long enough to see the person behind the role, understand what they need to feel valued, and respond accordingly. However, this requires something that our culture is rapidly losing: patience. What is behind the stories I've been telling? Patience. The willingness to have conversations that take longer than necessary. The ability to sit in silence while someone figures out what they really want to say. The discipline to put down your phone and pay attention to the person in front of you. And like the other human intelligence skills I've mentioned, patience is a skill that can be learned. It's not easy, but nothing worth doing ever is.

The people who learn to be patient, to see people's hopes and respond to them accordingly, don't just become better at their jobs; they become the kind of people who others want to work with, buy from, and build relationships with.

# THE RIGHT TOOLS FOR THE JOB | 7

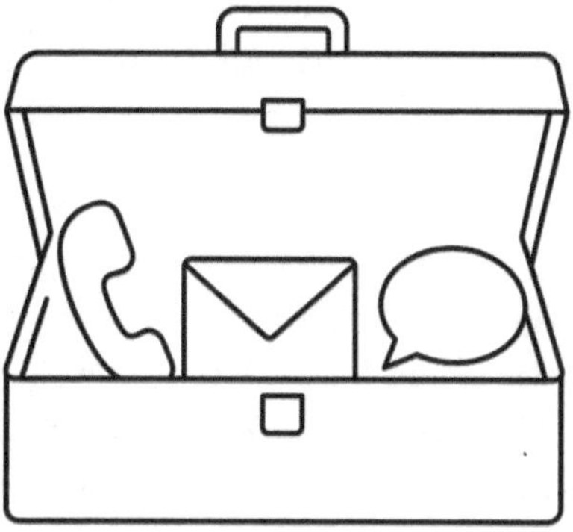

Fundamentally, the same skills that helped my parents in their in-person jobs and that Nat uses in the classroom are the same skills we need to navigate our digital-first world today. But we must *adapt* them to work through our screens and keyboards. Not because digital communication is bad in itself, but because different situations require different tools, and we must know which tools to use for which job.

Remember my meeting in Dublin that went wrong? Experiences like that taught me that reading the room in digital spaces isn't just about interpreting the signals as best you can but also recognising when those signals are telling you to shift to a different channel entirely. Part of being able to connect with people is knowing which channel is the best medium for that connection.

But here's the thing: Most people don't think about their communication tools strategically. They use whatever channel is most convenient or commonly used without considering whether it's the right medium for what they're trying to accomplish. Email for almost everything. Video calls for all meetings. Slack or something similar for urgent requests.

The truth is: Each channel has its own strengths and limitations, and the people who become skilled at digital relationship-building learn to choose the right medium depending on what they are trying to achieve.

The way I see it, there are two main channels: digital and human. Digital includes emails, video calls, AI, and instant messaging services like Slack. Human includes in-person, phone calls, and voice notes. Now I know that *technically* phone calls and voice notes are delivered by digital devices, but the difference is in efficiency vs effectiveness. As we saw in the previous chapter, phone calls are often more effective when it comes to human communication.

I use digital channels for what they're good at: efficiency. That means sharing information, coordinating logistics, and documenting decisions. I use human channels for what they're good at: effectiveness. That means building relationships, solving complex problems, resolving conflicts, developing real understanding, and creating trust.

Email is great for sharing information and documenting decisions, but terrible for building trust or resolving conflicts. Video calls are good for group coordination and presentations but limited for deep one-on-one conversations. Slack is perfect for quick check-ins and logistics, but awful for anything requiring nuance or emotional intelligence.

So, instead of trying to force all communication through digital channels, the key is to match the medium to the message, and to always be willing to escalate to a human channel if and when the situation requires it. This principle has transformed the way I work with global teams.

I now have a rule: If I can't understand what someone really needs after two digital interactions, I set up a phone call or send a Slack voice note so they can hear my voice and tone, then ask them to voice note-me back. That way, I can listen to what they're saying and not saying, just like my dad used to.

The result is that remote relationships feel more personal, projects run more smoothly, and problems get resolved before they become crises. Most importantly, people feel more connected to their work and to each other, even when they're separated by thousands of miles.

A few months ago, I was working with one of our partners in Australia on a high-stakes deal. We'd been exchanging emails for days trying to align on timelines, implementation plans, and approvals. The tone of the messages started to shift–short sentences, curt replies, and lots of "per my last email" energy. I could feel the tension rising, even though I wasn't sure why.

At one point, I reread a message three times, trying to decide whether they were being defensive or just direct. I realised how easy it is for meaning to get lost in translation: between cultures, time zones, and even punctuation marks. So, I decided to stop the back-and-forth. I picked up the phone at 7am Irish time from under my daughter's Peppa Pig quilt to call the partner. I had to make this phone call happen and time zones made it hard, so I made it work.

The moment I heard the partner's voice, everything changed. They weren't frustrated, just overwhelmed and worried that they'd misunderstood our internal process. Within fifteen minutes, we'd cleared up three days' worth of confusion, shared a laugh, and come up with a better plan. I followed up later with a short recap email, but the real work–the real connection–happened on that call.

Since then, I've stuck to my rule: After two digital exchanges without clarity, I move to voice, because sometimes the difference between friction and flow is simply hearing another human being speak.

This principle isn't about rejecting tech or AI tools but using them more strategically. The goal isn't for us to have fewer digital interactions or for them to be more efficient, but to have better interactions.

The companies that figure this out will have a massive advantage in our increasingly digital world. They'll be able to build trust across distances, resolve conflicts quickly, and create relationships that make complex collaborations possible. And for that, they'll need a range of tools in their belt. But as we've seen, tools alone are not enough–we also need the skills to enable human connection.

# RUTHLESS AUTOMATION | 8

In late 2024, I was on a call with one of our partners that left me feeling a bit unsettled. The partner was brilliant–absolutely brilliant–and he was walking me through his plans for using AI in his agency. His enthusiasm was contagious, and on the surface, everything sounded wonderful.

"We're going to automate nearly everything," he said, clicking through screen after screen of impressive dashboards. "AI will handle the client conversations, the analysis, the recommendations, and the follow-ups. We'll eliminate the mistakes that come from people being, well, people."

The services were genuinely impressive, the potential cost savings were substantial, and the efficiency gains were undeniable. But as I sat there listening, something didn't sit right with me. I kept thinking about the partners I'd worked with who had built lasting relationships with their clients, enabling them to weather tough times and get recommended to friends. They'd used technology to give them more time for the human stuff, not less.

This partner was heading down a different path entirely. He was so focused on making everything faster and more efficient that I feared he was about to automate away the very things that had made his agency successful in the first place. He was falling into what I've come to call *ruthless automation*. This is the idea that if we can just make our systems clever enough, we can eliminate the messy, unpredictable, gloriously human parts of working with people. And it comes with a big risk, as the partner soon found out.

Six months later, I had another call with him. The results weren't what he'd hoped for. His clients were drifting away. His team was feeling frustrated. And he was getting feedback that made him question everything, like, "You used to really understand our business. Now it feels like we're just talking to a computer."

The problem wasn't the AI he'd implemented. In fact, the technology was working exactly as it was supposed to. The problem was that he'd ruthlessly automated relationship-building along with everything else, and in the process had lost the human connections that made his agency special.

Before the automation, when a client rang up with a problem, they'd talk to Sarah, Michael, or David–team members who knew their business, remembered their last conversation, and knew what kept them up at night. The chat might have taken 20 minutes, but by the end of it, the client was confident that things would be fine.

What was really happening in those 20-minute conversations was something invisible but incredibly valuable: What the AI industry calls *decision threads* were being created with each interaction.

In the partner's case these weren't formal documents or checklists. They were the living history of how decisions had been made before–why for example an exception was granted, why a recommendation was softened, why one approach worked for this client but failed for another. Each conversation added another layer of understanding about the client, their context, and how best to serve them.

While the partner wasn't aware, those decision threads lived in his people–in memory, judgement, and experience. They were reinforced every time a human revisited a situation and thought, "Last time, this worked... but only because of X."

After the ruthless automation, the same client could get their answer in 3 minutes flat. The system could analyse their situation instantly and provide spot-on recommendations. It was faster, more accurate, and available around the clock. But it had no idea who they were as people, what mattered to them, or how to make them feel like they were in good hands.

The AI had access to data, but it had no access to those decision threads. It knew *what* had happened before, but not *why*. It couldn't see the trade-offs that had been debated, the emotional signals that had changed the direction of a conversation, or the context behind past decisions. And without those threads, it couldn't build a true understanding of the relationship.

It couldn't create the kind of connection that made them keep going back for years. And this is a big risk for businesses. Customers and clients don't just want their problems solved easily or their questions answered quickly–they want to know that the business genuinely cares about them, not just about getting a monthly retainer. And that can't be automated, no matter how clever AI gets. (We'll look at the reasons why humans want this in the next chapter.)

This is the trap I see businesses falling into, perhaps increasingly in the future. Leaders are getting so excited about what AI can do that they are forgetting what *only people* can do. And in doing so, they're ruthlessly automating their way out of the very relationships that made them successful.

They're using AI to handle client conversations when they should be using it to prepare for better conversations. They're using AI to replace the human touch when they should be using it to create more time for personal attention. Ironically, this is also how businesses lose the raw material needed to build meaningful context for AI in the first place. Without humans making decisions, explaining their reasoning, and navigating edge cases, there are no decision threads to capture. And without decision threads, there's no way to build what they call context graphs–structured ways of connecting decisions, outcomes, and reasoning over time.

It goes deeper. What they (and us collectively) risk losing to AI isn't just jobs–it's the training ground where people learn to understand people. The pattern recognition that comes from dealing with hundreds of distinct personalities. The emotional intelligence that develops from navigating difficult conversations. The gut instinct that comes from seeing how different approaches work with different people.

Those human experiences are exactly what future AI systems need to learn from–but only if we preserve them. Context graphs don't start with technology; they start with humans doing the work, making judgement calls, and explaining their thinking.

With this pattern, we risk creating a generation of professionals who can manage technology brilliantly but will never learn to read a room or have real conversations with customers. Who can interpret reports but can't gather the stories behind the numbers. Who can implement recommendations but not deal with the messy, human realities that make those recommendations work or fail.

To clarify, the problem here isn't AI itself–it's that humans are using AI to avoid the genuine hard work of connecting with other humans. We're ruthlessly automating relationship-building instead of using automation to create more time for relationship-building. Really, the magic isn't in *replacing* human connection but in using AI to create more time for it.

Think about it this way. AI is brilliant at the repetitive stuff: crunching numbers, spotting patterns, and handling routine tasks. People are brilliant at the creative and relational stuff: reading between the lines and figuring out what someone really needs.

When humans do that work, they create those decision threads. When those threads are captured, they become context. And when context is connected over time, it becomes a context graph–something AI can actually learn from instead of blindly executing rules.

Ruthless automation is real, and it's tempting. But it's risky and it's not effective as a long-term strategy. So, when you're strategising for the future, remember that AI should be used as a tool to *amplify* human capabilities, not replace them. Use it to handle the routine work but keep the human work for humans, otherwise you risk losing your customers–the people who keep you in business.

And this is where context graphs quietly come into the picture. They represent the missing why and how behind decisions–the connective tissue that explains not just what happened, but how people arrived there. AI can gather the data points and even produce the right answer, but without that context it doesn't truly understand the decision itself.

People are the same way: We don't trust conclusions unless we understand the reasoning behind them. And crucially, that reasoning doesn't appear on its own. It's created through human judgement, debate, mistakes, and lived experience. AI can learn from those decision threads, but it cannot create them in isolation. Whoever figures out how to capture and connect that human context–without stripping out the humanity that creates it–will give AI the understanding it's been missing. And whoever does that well will win.

In the next chapter, we'll look at what customers truly value and why they keep coming back.

# TRUST IN THE AGE OF ALGORITHMS | 9

The first time I truly understood what trust means in the digital age was during a conversation with my neighbour, Seamus, about online banking. Seamus was in his seventies, had been banking with the Bank of Ireland for forty years, and knew everyone by name in the local branch. When the bank moved most of its services online, he reluctantly learned to use the digital system. It was faster, available 24/7, and could handle most of his routine transactions with no human interaction.

"It's brilliant, really," he told me. "I can check my balance, pay bills, transfer money–all from my kitchen table. Much more convenient than driving into town." Then he paused. "The problem is, I don't trust it the way I trusted Mary."

Mary had been his banker for fifteen years. She knew his financial situation, understood his concerns about his pension, and had helped him navigate several complicated situations over the years. When Seamus had a question about a transaction, Mary didn't just provide the information, she made sure he understood it. When he was worried about a large expense, she helped him think through the implications.

The online system was automated and so could process his transactions faster and more accurately than Mary ever could. But it couldn't build the relationship that made Seamus feel confident about his financial decisions.

"With Mary, I knew she was looking out for me," Seamus said. "With the computer, I know it's just following its programming."

This conversation happened in 2019, but it feels more relevant now than ever. As AI systems become increasingly sophisticated and handle more of our daily interactions, the question of trust becomes more complex. We can build systems that are faster, more accurate, and more efficient than humans. But can we build systems that people trust? I don't think so. And more importantly, I don't think we should try.

The thing is: Trust isn't just about speed or competence–it's about the belief that someone truly cares for you, that when things go wrong someone will advocate for you. And going back to my early days of working in bars, it's about feeling heard, understood, and valued, not just *served*. In essence, it's about how we *feel*.

These things: someone having your best interests at heart, having your back, and being in good hands (notice the bodily words associated with this concept) are fundamentally human qualities that cannot be replicated by algorithms, no matter how sophisticated they become.

Yes, an AI system can process your data, predict your needs, and provide accurate recommendations to you, but it cannot care about you or your success the way a human can because it is not a human. It is transactional, not relational, and humans do not like to feel that they are being treated as merely a transaction. It can't understand what it feels like to be in someone else's situation. It can't respond with true empathy. And so it can't develop a trusting relationship in the same way that humans can.

The investment company I use to plan for my future has built an impressive AI system for investment advice. The system can analyse market conditions, assess risk tolerance, and provide personalised recommendations. But I'm still unsure. The issue isn't with the quality of the advice–it's the experience of receiving it. I feel like I'm interacting with a sophisticated calculator rather than a trusted adviser. There's that word *feel* again.

You see, research shows that people need to feel understood and valued. This happens through what psychologists call *empathic responding*: the ability to accurately perceive and respond to another person's emotional state.

Nat demonstrates this every day in her classroom. She can tell when a student's poor performance isn't about laziness but about something happening at home. She can read the difference between confusion and frustration, between shyness and disengagement.

Remember how she called her students weekly during COVID? She was tapping into one of the most important insights from neuroscience that trust is built through consistency and predictability. When people know what to expect from you because your actions align with your words and you respond to their needs reliably, their brains literally rewire to see you as trustworthy. Her students expected that weekly phone call checking they were okay.

The people who excel at building relationships–whether they're teachers, parents, community guards, or business partners–have developed sophisticated skills in empathic responding. They can read the emotional subtext of conversations, understand what someone needs even when they can't articulate it clearly, and respond in ways that make people feel heard and valued. This is what I'd observed my family doing when I was a child.

When my father checked in on the senior residents, they knew he'd stop by regularly, not because he had to but because he genuinely cared about their welfare. The shopkeepers knew he'd regularly ask about their families and remember details from previous conversations. This consistency created the foundation of trust that made his real police work possible.

I see this playing out in my own work now. The partners who trust me most aren't necessarily the ones I've known longest; they're the ones who've seen me consistently deliver on small commitments over time. They've learned that when I say I'll follow up on something, it happens. When I commit to a call time, I'm there. When I promise to connect them with someone, I do. This consistency creates a psychological safety that makes everything else possible. When people trust that you'll follow through, they're more willing to share sensitive information, take risks, and collaborate on complex projects.

This can't be done in a transactional way as trust is built through relationships. This means that every interaction is an opportunity to demonstrate competence, reliability, and genuine care for the other person. And that is something AI can't do.

As I've said before, this doesn't mean that AI is bad, or that we should avoid using it. It just means that we need to be thoughtful about how and where we deploy it, especially in situations where building trust is essential to our partners, clients, or customers.

In doing so, we need to recognise that trust operates on multiple levels. Yes, people need to practically trust that they're getting good advice quickly (which AI can provide), but they also need to emotionally trust that someone cares about them (which only humans can do).

In healthcare, patients need to trust they're getting accurate diagnoses and effective treatments. But they also need to trust that their concerns are being heard and they're being treated with dignity and compassion.

With legal services, clients need to trust that they're getting competent representation but also trust that the lawyer understands their situation and will advocate for their best interests.

In customer service, people need to trust that their problems will be resolved efficiently, but also that they're being treated fairly and someone will take responsibility if things go wrong.

AI can support these practical needs, but it can't replace the human elements that make trust possible: the emotional ones. And that's why the most successful companies will be those that use AI to automate the transactional stuff to create more time for humans to do the human stuff.

For example, with my investment advisors, AI could handle the analysis, research, and initial recommendations, but every client would have a human adviser who understands their personal situation, explains AI's recommendations in plain language, and is available for nuanced conversations about their money that build trust over time.

Likewise, the medical practice could use AI to handle appointment scheduling, insurance verification, and initial symptom assessment, then use the time savings so doctors can spend more time with their patients, really listening to their concerns and explaining treatment options in detail.

The law firm might use AI to review documents, research case law, and draft initial versions of standard legal documents, then use the efficiency gains to provide more strategic advice to clients and to be more responsive to complex questions. Their clients will feel better served because the lawyers can focus on the high-value activities that require human judgement.

The consulting firm might use AI to analyse market data, identify trends, and prepare initial recommendations, then use the insights to have more strategic conversations with clients about long-term planning and risk management. Their relationships will deepen because they can spend more time on advisory work rather than information gathering.

However, this requires a fundamental shift in how we think about the role of AI in business. Instead of asking, "What can we automate?" we need to ask, "How can we use automation to create more value for the people we serve?"

The companies that do this will be the ones that people trust with their most important decisions, sensitive problems, and most valuable relationships. The ones customers choose to work with, employees choose to stay at, and partners choose to collaborate with. The future belongs to organisations that understand this balance and use it to create competitive advantages, remembering that the goal isn't to respond faster but to understand people better. This is where human intelligence becomes irreplaceable.

# CONNECTION CAPITAL | 10

My grandfather had a theory about people that shaped how I think about business relationships to this day. He used to say, "Everyone has a story that would break your heart and a story that would make you proud. Your job is to find both."

He was a farmer, but he could have been a master negotiator or a skilled therapist. He had an ability to connect with people that went beyond surface-level pleasantries. Whether he was hiring seasonal workers, dealing with suppliers, or sorting out disputes between neighbours, he approached every interaction with a genuine curiosity about the person he was talking to.

My dad told me about a farm labourer who showed up looking rough around the edges, wearing clothes that had seen better days, and with a nervousness that suggested he really needed the work. Most employers would have made a quick decision based on appearances. But my grandfather spent an hour talking to him, learning about his family situation, previous experiences, and aspirations. While he was skilled at determining a person's work ethic quickly based on how fast they ate, he also knew when something required a longer, more in-depth exploration.

By the end of that conversation, he'd learned this man had been laid off from another job through no fault of his own, was supporting his elderly mother, and had grown up on a farm but hadn't worked the land in years. He was nervous because he cared about doing a good job, not because he was unreliable.

My grandfather hired him on the spot, and that man worked for him for the next five years. He became not just an employee but a friend, someone who would go out of his way to help during busy periods and whose local knowledge helped avoid several expensive mistakes.

More importantly, that relationship became the foundation for a network of connections and insights that served the farm for decades. My grandfather had built what I now call *connection capital*.

Connection capital is about building relational assets that appreciate over time, and investing in authentic connections that create returns far beyond individual transactions. It's the difference between having business contacts and people you can bank on when it matters most.

He probably wouldn't have called it "connection capital", but my grandfather understood this instinctively. He didn't just hire the labourer and move on. He invested time in remembering details like the man's mother's health, asking about his children's schooling, and staying connected to his broader life context. When harvest time came and he needed additional help, the labourer knew exactly who to recommend. When equipment broke down, he knew who could fix it quickly at a fair price. When weather threatened the crops, he had insights about timing that saved lots of money. Those weren't transactions but investments that compounded over time.

I see this same principle playing out in modern business, but most organisations are terrible at it. They treat relationships like checking accounts–making deposits only when they need withdrawals. But connection capital works like an investment portfolio–making consistent deposits over time, which creates exponential returns that no single transaction could generate.

However, building connection capital requires us to shift from reactive relationship management to proactive relationship investment. This means instead of waiting for people to need something *from you*, you're constantly looking for ways to add value *for them*.

The companies I work with that truly understand this don't just maintain client relationships–they systematically invest in them. They have what I call the 3-2-1 investment system with key relationships: 3 non-transactional touchpoints per quarter, 2 pieces of valuable content shared proactively (articles, introductions, insights), 1 personal milestone remembered and acknowledged.

This might sound like a transactional checklist, but it's actually a mindset. They're genuinely curious about their clients' lives, industry challenges, and personal and professional goals. They send articles that might interest them, make introductions that could be valuable, and stay in touch even during periods when there's no active project.

Building connection capital has become both easier and harder in our digital age. Easier because we have more ways to stay connected across distance and time. Harder because digital interactions can feel transactional even when they're meant to be relational. And harder because it sometimes doesn't feel efficient or beneficial for the bottom line in the short term.

By its very nature, it involves providing value without the expectation of immediate reciprocation. Sometimes, that means offering insights, introductions, and resources that help the person succeed and never seeing those return. Often, they return later down the line, and sometimes in abundance.

Of course, this also means maintaining connection continuity across project cycles and organisational changes, such as staff moving on. It requires businesses to build relationship depth with multiple stakeholders within important organisations, not just one of your team having a great business relationship with one of their team, and then one or the other leaves and the whole organisational relationship breaks down.

This is why a wise business owner maps the relationship networks within their key client organisations. They don't just know the person who hired them–they know the broader stakeholder ecosystem and invest in relationships across multiple levels. When organisational changes happen, they're not starting from scratch because they built connection capital throughout the system.

The most powerful aspect of connection capital is how it multiplies over time. Each strong relationship connects you to that person's network, creating an exponential expansion of opportunities. One well-invested relationship can open doors to dozens of additional connections.

But this only works when the investment is genuine. People can sense when you're building relationships for your own benefit and when you're genuinely interested in their success. The difference is in your motivation: Are you trying to extract value from this relationship, or create value for this person?

My grandfather hired that labourer not because he calculated the network effects, but because he cared about giving someone a chance to succeed. The compound returns–the referrals, insights, and loyalty–all happened naturally because the foundation was built on something genuine.

In our AI-enhanced world, this principle becomes even more important. As technology handles more routine interactions, the ability to build genuine human connections becomes increasingly valuable. The organisations that invest systematically in connection capital will find themselves with networks they can rely on when markets shift, when challenges arise, and when opportunities emerge.

At the end of the day, business is still about people choosing to work with people they trust. And that requires the choice to invest in others' success, even when there's no immediate benefit to yourself. That's connection capital, and it's the foundation of every relationship worth banking on (pardon the pun).

# HUMANS IN THE LOOP | 11

Recently, an inevitable call came in. One of our most important partners was in crisis, and not a technical crisis but a human one. Their team was burned out, their clients were frustrated, and relationships that had taken years to build were falling apart in a matter of weeks.

"We've automated everything we can," the founder told me. "Our systems are more efficient than ever. But somehow, we're losing the human connection that made us successful in the first place. How do we scale care?"

It's a question I hear constantly from business leaders: How do you maintain the human elements that drive success while building systems that can grow? How do you create frameworks that are both scalable and genuinely caring?

The answer took me back to two experiences that taught me everything I know about building systems that amplify human connection: my time in the Reserve Army and setting up a charity in Kenya. They taught me what I now call *empathic structuring*: creating frameworks that systematically balance care with accountability.

I was 22, standing in a field in Finner Camp in Donegal, trying to figure out how to march a section of soldiers without walking them straight into a wall, again. It was my first real leadership test in the Reserve Army's 5th Field Signals, and I was failing spectacularly. I'd been promoted to corporal, which meant I was responsible for getting thirty other people from point A to point B in formation. Simple enough in theory. In practice, I'd already marched my platoon into a fence, led them in a perfect circle back to where we started, and on one memorable occasion, called "left turn" when I meant "right turn" and watched them march directly toward the canteen.

A sergeant, who'd been watching this disaster unfold with amused patience, finally called me over.

"McDevitt," he said, "you're not thinking ahead. Leadership isn't just about giving commands; it's about anticipating problems and guiding your team around obstacles, not into them. Take some responsibility."

Responsibility and accountability are reinforced by the buddy system. From day one of training, recruits were paired together. Your success was connected to theirs. If their uniforms weren't perfect, you both failed the inspection. If they fell behind on a march, you helped them keep up. If you succeeded and they didn't, you hadn't really succeeded at all.

My buddy, Sinéad, had never done anything remotely military in her life. She was brilliant at the technical communications work we were training for, but she struggled with the physical demands and strict routine. I could have focused solely on my own performance, but the system made it clear that wasn't an option.

So, I started paying attention to what she needed. I noticed she performed better when she had time to prepare for inspections, so I'd help her lay out her kit the night before. I saw that she got nervous during drills when she couldn't remember sequences, so we'd practice together until it became automatic. I learned to read her stress signals and offer support before she got overwhelmed.

This is precisely what the best business partnerships do. They create systems where everyone's success is interconnected. When one client struggles, the whole team mobilises to help. When one team member is overwhelmed, others step in, not because they're required to, but because the framework makes mutual support the natural response.

The buddy system taught me that you can have both structure and flexibility, discipline and compassion. The framework created space for both care and accountability. When Sinéad wasn't putting in an effort, I had to address it directly. When I was letting the team down, she called me on it.

The business application became clear years later when I started working with companies struggling to scale their client relationships. The most successful ones had created "buddy systems" for their clients–structured approaches that ensured no client relationship depended on a single person, while maintaining the personal connection that clients valued.

The military taught me about *systematic accountability*, and then I learned about *systematic care* through my work with

Help Us Give Smiles (HUGS), a charity I established to support Terry's Youth and Resource Centre in Kenya.

It started with good intentions and naive assumptions. Like many Westerners, I thought charity work was about giving money and directing solutions. But when I met Leah Ambwaya, who runs the Terry Child Support Foundation for vulnerable children, I understood what I'd been missing. Leah had solved the same problem that modern businesses struggle with–how to create systems that can scale care without losing authenticity.

The first time I visited Terry's, I was struck by how different it felt from other projects I'd seen. There was structure, but it didn't feel rigid. There were rules, but they felt supportive rather than punitive. The children were clearly thriving, but they also understood what was expected of them.

Leah had created what I now recognise as a masterclass in empathic structuring. She'd built frameworks that addressed both the practical needs of running a children's centre and the emotional needs of children who'd experienced trauma and abandonment.

Every child at Terry's had a daily routine that included school, chores, and free time. But the routine was flexible enough to accommodate individual needs; some children needed more structure; others needed more freedom. Some responded well to group activities; others needed one-on-one attention. And she knew that certain children would need extra structure during transitions.

The rules at Terry's were clear and consistent, but they were explained in terms of caring for each other rather than arbitrary restrictions. Children understood that showing up for meals on time wasn't just about efficiency but not making the cooks worry. Keeping dormitories clean wasn't just about hygiene but creating a space that everyone could feel proud of.

When problems arose, Leah had structured approaches that addressed both the immediate issue and the underlying needs. If a child was acting out, she didn't just impose consequences, she looked for what the behaviour was trying to communicate. Was the child feeling overwhelmed? Left out? Worried about something? The response addressed both the behaviour and the need behind it.

Every successful business I work with today operates on the same principles. Have strong values but adaptable processes. They have standardised processes that ensure consistency and quality, but they adapt those processes based on each client's working style, communication preferences, and business context. The goal is to meet people where they are, not force them into rigid frameworks that don't serve their actual needs.

They have clear communication protocols that establish how decisions are made, how problems escalate, and how feedback is shared as this reduces anxiety and builds trust.

When a client becomes difficult or demanding, the best account managers don't just manage the symptoms–they investigate what's driving the behaviour. Often, *difficult* clients are just worried clients, overwhelmed clients, or clients who feel unheard. They also build frameworks that address anticipated needs before they become urgent problems. Great account managers know when clients will need additional support during busy seasons or organisational changes. This is the gold standard for client relationship management.

Compare this to companies that create policies focused on compliance rather than care. Their employee handbooks read like legal documents. Their client contracts emphasise limitations rather than commitments. The best organisations flip this–their systems explicitly exist to take better care of people.

When I decided to formalise HUGS as a charity, I found myself drawing on both my Reserve Army experience and what I'd learned from watching Leah work. I knew that good intentions and fundraising weren't enough. I needed to create structures that could sustain support over time, handle the complexities of cross-cultural collaboration, and create accountability for everyone involved.

In the early days, volunteers who traveled with me to Kenya would get swept up in the emotional experience and want to make promises that weren't sustainable–sponsoring individual children, funding specific projects, maintaining ongoing relationships. Their hearts were in the right place, but I'd learned from Leah that creating expectations you can't meet is more harmful than not making promises at all.

We developed *volunteer commitments*: clear guidelines about what volunteers could and couldn't promise, structured ways to follow through on commitments that were made, and systems for maintaining relationships that were realistic given the constraints of distance and resources.

Instead of just sending money and hoping for the best, we created structured communication systems–regular reports, photo updates, and specific funding agreements. But these structures were designed to build trust and understanding, not to create bureaucratic burden.

We learned that transparency and accountability strengthened relationships rather than undermined them. When everyone understood how decisions were made, where money was going, and what results we were achieving, there was more trust and collaboration, not less.

The most successful businesses do exactly this. They create frameworks that channel enthusiasm in ways that are helpful rather than just emotionally satisfying. They build systems that make it easier to under-promise and over-deliver rather than the reverse.

The companies with the strongest client loyalty aren't the ones that hide problems or present everything as perfect. They're the ones that create systematic transparency about process, progress, and challenges.

Compare this to sales teams that overpromise to close deals, account managers who commit to timelines they can't meet, or leaders who create expectations about company direction without considering resource constraints. This approach only leaves people feeling disappointed.

What I learned from the Reserve Army and HUGS is that the best way to take care of people systematically is to create systems that anticipate their needs, provide clear and honest support, and maintain appropriate boundaries.

The companies I work with that have mastered empathic structuring don't see systems and relationships as opposing forces but tools for scaling authentic care. Because at the end of the day, the question isn't whether you'll have systems in your business–*you will*. The question is whether these systems will amplify or diminish your ability to genuinely care for the people you serve. Empathic structuring ensures that as you grow, you become more caring, not less.

# 12 PATTERN RECOGNITION

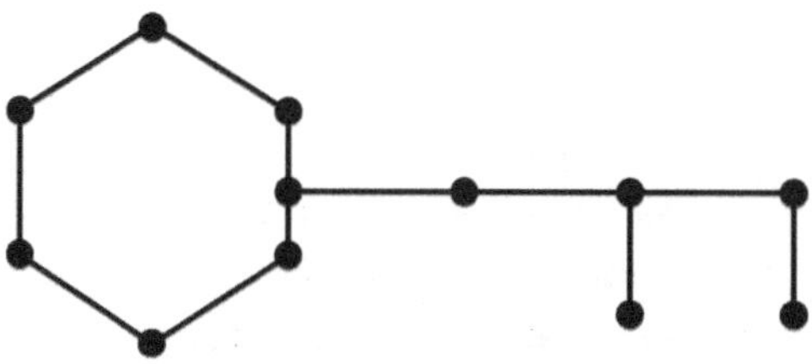

"You've been telling me stories about reading people and building relationships for as long as I've known you," my wife Geraldine said one evening as I was complaining about how hard it was to explain why relationships mattered in business. "Stories from when you were eight years old, stories from Kenya, stories from the army, stories from every job you've ever had. Have you ever considered that maybe you're not trying to convince people of something new; maybe you're trying to help them remember something they've forgotten?"

She was right, and it stung a bit. But more importantly, she'd identified the pattern I'd been missing: The skills that made me successful weren't unique to me–they were human capabilities that would help any business succeed, capabilities that our business culture had systematically undervalued.

This realisation hit me just as I was watching companies struggle with the fundamental question: "How do you compete when AI can handle most of the technical tasks that used to differentiate you?"

The morning after my conversation with Geraldine, I had a call with a partner who was panicking about AI disruption. "Our competitors are automating everything," he said. "They're faster, cheaper, and more consistent than we are. How do we compete?"

This was exactly the situation I'd faced at that round table in 1989. The "smart" kids at the triangle and square tables could memorise information quickly and spit it back accurately. They were the human equivalent of efficient processing systems.

Those of us relegated to the round table had developed unique skills because we had to. We'd learned to read moods, read the room, read between the lines, and read different personalities, then adapt our approach accordingly and find creative solutions when conventional ones didn't work. Now, the conventional skills were becoming automated and the round table skills were becoming invaluable.

"Here's the thing," my wife said, "AI is about to put everyone in a round table position like you were. The standard approaches like following a script, processing information faster, treating meetings like transactions… those won't give anyone an advantage anymore. The question will be: What are your round table skills?"

This conversation led me to think more about the most successful people I knew across different industries. The pattern was clear: They all had what I think of as the skill of *pattern recognition* for human complexity. This is what Geraldine was hinting at when she said "something they've forgotten".

Pattern recognition is knowing enough about the past to predict what's coming in the future based on a collection of events or behaviours. On the logical side, this could be patterns of numbers like economic cycles. On the emotional side, this could be noticing people's reactions to things. In other words, it's the lived experience of knowing what's coming next as you've seen it before. This pattern recognition is what underpins our sense of intuition, which is far less mystical than it might seem.

The account managers who retained clients the longest weren't the ones who responded fastest to emails but who recognised the patterns of a client's speech and reactions, so when they said, "We need this campaign to be perfect," the account manager understood, "We're under pressure from leadership, my neck is on the line, and I need to feel confident about this decision." Their response addressed both what they said the need was (quality work) and the unspoken need (reassurance and involvement in the process).

The managers with the highest-performing teams weren't the most technically skilled but the ones who could recognise patterns in team members' working styles, motivation, and stress signals. From these patterns, they knew which team members needed detailed direction versus high-level goals, who performed better with public recognition versus private feedback, and when performance issues were capacity problems rather than capability problems.

The sales reps with the highest close rates weren't the ones with the best pitch or demo but the ones who could recognise the patterns in prospect situations and adapt their approach accordingly. From these patterns, they could tell the difference between a prospect who needed deep details versus one who needed strategic vision, someone who was genuinely interested opposed to just being polite, and objections that were real concerns versus negotiation and discount tactics.

The people who created the most valuable long-term relationships weren't the most aggressive networkers but the ones who could recognise the patterns in real common ground and mutual value. From these patterns, they could identify who the real decision-makers were, what each stakeholder needed to feel comfortable moving forward, and what each person needed to strengthen their relationship.

What Geraldine reminded me is that AI isn't creating the need for these skills–it's just reminding people how valuable they've always been. Companies that have previously relied on efficiency, speed, and technical competence are suddenly finding themselves commoditised as AI handles those functions better than humans ever could. By contrast, companies that have built their success on recognising human patterns are discovering that AI amplifies rather than threatens their competitive advantage.

Before AI, a consulting firm competed on their ability to analyse data and identify trends faster than their competitors. With AI, every consulting firm has access to the same capabilities. The differentiator is the ability to recognise the patterns in specific client situations, organisational dynamics, and strategic constraints that don't show up in data.

Before AI, an agency won clients by demonstrating technical expertise and creative capabilities. With AI, technical execution becomes table stakes. The differentiator is the ability to recognise the patterns in what clients really need beyond what they're asking for and build the relationships that enable truly strategic partnerships.

Before AI, a software company competed on feature functionality and system performance, and that will remain true in some ways. With AI, software product capabilities will rapidly become comparable across competitors. The differentiator is recognising the patterns in client interactions that signify the level of implementation support required, and the nuanced solutions needed.

This idea of pattern recognition brings together everything I've been talking about: the ability to read, understand, and respond effectively in human interactions. Deconstructing human communication made me realise that it naturally forms into layers of meaning:

**Layer 1, Surface Communication:** This is what people say–the literal content of communications. AI can process this perfectly.

**Layer 2, Emotional Context:** This is how people feel about what they're saying. AI can identify some emotional indicators, but human pattern recognition is superior at interpreting complex emotional states and their implications.

**Layer 3, Situational Dynamics:** This is what's really happening in the broader context. This requires an understanding of organisational politics, personal pressures, industry dynamics, and relationship histories that AI cannot fully grasp.

**Layer 4, Unspoken Needs:** This is what people need versus what they're asking for. This level requires intuitive leaps, creative problem-solving, and the ability to connect seemingly unrelated pieces of information. AI struggles with this.

**Layer 5, Relationship Investment:** This is the understanding of how to build trust and mutual value over time. This requires long-term thinking, values-based judgement, and the ability to prioritise relationship health over short-term gains. AI cannot do this.

*Values-based judgement* is the ability to unite different data points to make a judgement. On the one hand, we have logical data points, like: Does it make money? Is it going to cause people to lose their jobs? Is it detrimental to the brand? On the other hand, we have emotional data points, like: Does it hurt people? Will it stop someone from paying their mortgage? Will it damage the environment? Values-based judgement is where these data points converge, where we consider both elements when making a decision.

The people who excel at layers 3–5 of meaning create a sustainable competitive advantage that AI cannot replicate. And the beauty of this is people who struggle with layers 1-2 can still succeed. As a neurodivergent person (like many of us at that round table), this is important. Some of us struggle with layers 1 or 2, or both. Maybe we need direct communication and can't read between the lines of implied speech. Maybe we struggle to label emotions.

But perhaps we're great at recognising patterns in body language or tone of voice that signal a change in energy. Perhaps we excel at catching contradictions between what someone is saying and their facial expression. In fact, many neurodivergent people have enhanced pattern recognition skills. However, these are human skills anyone can develop if they recognise their importance and practice them. And now, AI is about to make these skills necessary for everyone.

It's also important to note that with the increased understanding of neurodiversity, rooms are changing. We're becoming more aware that people process information, emotions, and social cues in vastly different ways and that diversity of thinking adds real value to teams and decisions, much like the round table.

But long before we had the language for neurodivergence (which wasn't around in my day!) many women were already navigating the world with an acute awareness of context, tone, and unspoken dynamics. They'd been reading rooms differently for generations. My grandmother told me stories of when she had to "put up and shut up" even in her world of 1950s Ireland.

For many women, this skill developed out of necessity and survival. When you're part of a group that has historically had to adapt to spaces not designed for you, you learn to pick up on micro-signals like who is comfortable, who is disengaged, who holds the power, and who is being overlooked. You start to listen not only to what's being said, but also to what isn't.

In particular, women of colour often carry an additional layer of perception. They're attuned to intersectional dynamics: the subtle interplay of race, gender, class, and hierarchy. Being entirely honest, this is something I've only educated myself on in recent years while working for an American company that values intersectionality, and because colleagues had given me feedback about things I had missed. For example, how they'd had to read whether it's safe to speak up, whether an idea would be received or dismissed, and whether a tone shift signalled curiosity or condescension.

However, this emotional and social intelligence isn't just survival but strategy. It enables people to develop and demonstrate empathy, foresight, and leadership in complex, cross-cultural, and hybrid environments. In an age when organisations prize emotional intelligence and inclusive leadership, these are precisely the skills that move teams forward.

So, as we widen our understanding of neurodiversity and human differences, we also need to recognise that these deep, often unacknowledged abilities like the capacity to read nuance, sense undercurrents, and anticipate reactions are *not* soft skills. They are hard-earned forms of intelligence that have always existed, particularly among those who've had to navigate the world differently.

# BUILDING RELATIONAL INTELLIGENCE | 13

Looking back at everything I've shared, from the round table in 1989 to the AI-powered conversations I'm having today, there is a thread running through it all. I didn't have a name for it back then—I just saw it as human intelligence. I also knew that these skills matter: in classrooms, communities, workplaces, charity work, and every context where people have to work together to achieve something meaningful. In 2026, I call it *relational intelligence*, or RI.

Why "relational"? Because it's about relationships. Human connection is built on relationships, and the flow of dynamics between people. While skills like emotional intelligence (EQ) have been promoted for decades, the focus on understanding and managing our own emotions can lead us to be too internal and insular. And as mentioned in the previous chapter, it can also be a challenge or hindrance for some neurodivergent people. As a result, EQ has been seen as a soft skill. By contrast, RI is broader, and is able to be developed and measured through five core signals.

Why "signals"? Again, because it's about the external and not just the internal. For decades, we've focused on developing skills, but this can lead us to be too insular. By contrast, signals involve not just the inward skill development but the external reflection of these skills in our interaction. Our signposting to the world that these things matter.

These signals are things that have underpinned the stories I've been telling you, and together they create a comprehensive approach to human connection in professional contexts.

## Signal 1: Presence

You might have noticed that presence has been an undercurrent running beneath every story, and particularly in chapter 3. If we want to create genuine human connections, then we have to be present. If we're not paying attention, then how can we notice patterns and pick up on subtle signals?

Presence is maintaining connection in the moment, even virtually. Being attentive and engaged in interactions, bringing your full attention without digital distractions, truly listening rather than just waiting for your turn to speak, and making others feel seen and heard–not just nodding and then going back to scrolling on your phone.

David has mastered this art. In any in-person business conversation, he puts away his phone, closes his laptop, and listens with his whole being. In the first few minutes he asks, "What's keeping you busy these days?" It's a simple question, but it opens possibilities that "How's business?" doesn't.

In response, people might talk about work challenges, but they also might mention family situations, personal interests, or concerns that have nothing to do with business. David listens for all of it, because he understands that truly connecting with someone as a person makes everything else easier, and that connection can't happen if you're only half-listening to the answer while checking your emails.

This presence creates a different energy in conversations, one that makes people want to share more and engage more deeply. And it enables David to be aware of and respond to emotional shifts in real time, creating the conditions where people feel understood and valued.

## Signal 2: Awareness

Like presence, awareness has been an undercurrent running through many of the stories, especially in chapters 2, 6, and 7. If we want to create genuine human connections, then we need to have a strong sense of awareness.

Awareness involves reading the tone, timing, and subtext of interactions. This awareness is what creates the ability to read a room—understanding what people need beyond what they explicitly say. People often don't say exactly what they mean. They hint and imply. They subtly communicate through tone and timing of what they say, and also the things they don't say. This will always be hard for AI to compete with, and this gives humans an advantage.

Practically, this capability might look like catching contradictions between what someone says and the way they say it. It might be noticing energy shifts or energy levels in group dynamics. And as a result of this awareness, you sense when it's time to push forward versus pull back.

Sarah runs a design agency, and she's become masterful at reading client signals. When a client says, "I trust your judgement, just send me something," she knows that this usually means the opposite–they're anxious about losing control and actually want more involvement, not less. So she knows to ask them more questions to uncover what they really want.

When a client gives feedback like, "It's nice, but something's not quite right," Sarah doesn't just ask for more specifics. She asks about the context: Who else will see this? What are you hoping this will accomplish? What are you worried about?

Nine times out of ten, the actual issue isn't with the design–it's with unstated concerns about how the design will be received by their boss, customers, or the board. By reading these signals, Sarah can address the actual problem instead of just the surface feedback.

Learning to read these subtle signals is like learning a second language–one that most people speak but few people consciously understand.

## Signal 3: Connection Capital

As you saw in chapter 9, connection capital means developing relational assets that appreciate over time, investing in authentic connections that create compound returns. This means building in regular, non-transactional check-ins, value-sharing proactively beyond contractual obligations, and systematically gathering knowledge about a client's broader context.

Catherine runs a small PR firm, and she has built her entire business model around this principle. She deliberately keeps her client roster small so she can maintain deep relationships with each client. She knows their businesses intimately, understands their strategic challenges, and often suggests solutions before problems become critical.

But Catherine's connection capital goes deeper than just knowing business details. She remembers personal milestones, industry challenges, and the details from their professional lives. She sends articles that might interest them, makes introductions that could be valuable, and stays in touch even during periods when there's no active project.

Her clients stay with her for years, refer new clients regularly, and pay premium rates because they trust her judgement completely. She's built a sustainable business by investing in relationships rather than just optimising for transaction volume.

This approach requires thoughtful relationship mapping across organisations rather than individual contacts, understanding that relationships require ongoing attention, not just attention when you need something.

## Signal 4: Empathic Structuring

As you saw in chapter 11, empathic structuring involves care and boundaries built into work. This means creating frameworks that balance support with accountability and creating guardrails with heart. It means creating clear rules of engagement that honour everyone's needs, designing feedback systems that balance honesty with care, and establishing decision frameworks that include both logical and emotional considerations.

Paul runs a consulting firm, and he has structured his client relationships. He has built systems that are both supportive and accountable. During onboarding, he creates explicit agreements about communication styles, decision-making processes, and feedback loops. He asks clients about their preferred working styles, stress signals, and what support looks like for them.

But Paul also builds in accountability structures. He sets clear expectations about timelines, deliverables, and mutual responsibilities. If projects start to drift, he has structured check-ins that address both the practical issues and the emotional dynamics that might cause them.

This empathic structuring has prevented countless relationship breakdowns. By anticipating human needs and building frameworks to address them, Paul creates environments where people can do their best work while maintaining healthy boundaries.

## Signal 5: Human Differentiation

Also underpinning a lot of these stories is the element of human differentiation, as mentioned in chapter 12. This means being different not just from AI, but from other humans. Human differentiation means bringing humanity that no AI or other human can replicate.

I first saw this back at the round table, that everyone is completely unique. Their lived experience, their individual qualities, their personal perspective. And as a result, the ideas they came up with and the way they solved problems. The intuition they developed through their experiences. And their own sense of values-based judgement.

I've also seen this throughout my career. I often joke with younger colleagues that the only real difference between someone with a career and someone just starting one is the number of mistakes the former has made and lived through. Every misstep becomes a data point. Over years, those experiences form a kind of human algorithm, one that's unique to each of us. That's *human differentiation*: No two people will ever solve a problem in the same way as they haven't lived the same lives.

Importantly, for this to work, we have to arrive as we are and be genuinely authentic in our individual selves. This authentic vulnerability creates psychological safety for others, which leads to better human connection. Early on in life, I discovered that some people found me entertaining. I say *some* because the truth is, I'm not for everyone. Some people like my humour, while others don't. And that's fine, because we're all unique individuals.

One of the biggest shifts in my career came when I stopped trying to sound like everyone else and started showing up as myself. For a long time, I thought professionalism meant polishing out the parts of me that were messy or complicated–the very things that made me human. But over time, I realised that my authentic self and my lived experiences were the foundation of how I solved problems, built relationships, and led teams.

There's one moment that stands out. I was managing a tricky customer situation that could have easily spiraled into conflict. Tensions were high and several people on the team were hesitant to be direct in fear of upsetting the client. But my instinct shaped by years of learning to face uncomfortable truths told me the fastest way to resolution was honesty. So I laid it all out clearly and calmly: what wasn't working, what we could fix, and what we needed from them in return. To my surprise, the customer thanked me. They said it was the first time someone had spoken to them so plainly. And that's when I realised: My directness wasn't a flaw. It was part of what made me effective.

That trait came from a deeply personal place. I didn't come out as a gay woman until I was 33. For years before that, I spent enormous energy trying to hide one big truth about myself. That experience shaped me, as I'd become so used to carrying a secret that I simply didn't have the capacity to carry any others. So I learned to be transparent. To say the thing that others were thinking but didn't want to voice. To save everyone the time and tension of dancing around what really mattered.

It's funny to think that the thing I once thought I had to hide became one of my greatest professional strengths. My lived experience taught me that honesty builds trust faster than anything else, and that being human, flawed, different, and real is what allows others to truly connect with you. Others understand that too.

Paul exemplifies this in his approach to client relationships. One of his human differentiators is being brutally honest about whether his services are the right fit for a potential client. He's turned down lucrative contracts because he didn't think he was the best person for the job–a decision that requires values-based judgement and long-term thinking, which AI cannot replicate.

This approach costs him money in the short term, but it's made him incredibly valuable in the long term. His clients trust his judgement completely because they know he'll tell them the truth even when it's not in his immediate interest. His authentic vulnerability creates psychological safety for his customers, which enables genuine problem-solving and innovation to occur.

The companies that thrive in the next decade will be those that value and reward the signals of RI. But this requires a fundamental shift in how we think about business success.

Instead of optimising purely for short-term efficiency, we need to optimise for long-term relationship health. Rather than viewing human connections as nice-to-haves, we need to see them as essential infrastructure for sustainable success. The question is: What if we don't? What happens to companies that don't believe in RI? And what happens to individuals who don't invest in developing these signals?

# THE FUTURE TEAM | 14

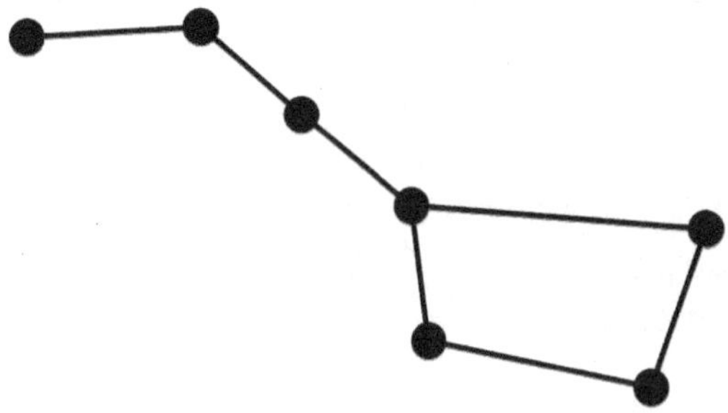

One night, my eight-year-old son Lochlan was sitting at the kitchen table, staring at his homework with the existential dread usually reserved for cleaning his room. Lochlan is my eldest, brother to his younger siblings Grayson, Willow, and Cooper. So, he's experiencing everything first.

"Mum," he said, "why do I have to do this? Can't I just ask the Jackie-GT?" I laughed because, honestly, it's a fair question. Lochlan can already use AI to help with research on sea creatures, explain complex concepts, or even generate tailored jokes. He's growing up in a world where information is infinite and instantly accessible. So why learn maths when AI can do the addition faster?

I didn't want to do my homework as a kid either, but things are different now. When I was eight, sitting at that round table feeling like I wasn't worth the effort, at least the path forward was somewhat predictable. Do well in school, get good final exam results, go to university, get a job, and work your way up.

The system was flawed, but it was clear. Lochlan and other kids today face a far less certain path. Traditional careers and educational pathways have been thrown into question. The jobs they'll do might not exist yet, and the skills needed are still being discovered. The very nature of work is evolving faster than our ability to prepare them for it. For a moment, I thought... What will he do in the future? What will jobs look like when he's 25? What skills will he need? Will traditional employment even exist in the way we see it now?

Obviously, he still needs to learn to think, and homework is good practice for that. But I find myself asking: What will give him an advantage in an AI-first world? I know it will be his ability to influence and connect. Lochlan knows everyone in his school–from the guy who delivers the milk to all the teaching assistants, from the principal to the kids in junior infants. He remembers their names, asks about their families, and somehow makes everyone feel like they matter. Not sure where he gets it from!

He's naturally big on connection in a way that no algorithm can replicate. But here's the thing that makes me laugh–he can use AI to write stories, solve maths problems, and research any topic under the sun, but he genuinely cannot understand where clean laundry comes from.

He's growing up in a world where AI handles complex cognitive tasks while basic human skills like understanding people, building relationships, and creating trust become increasingly rare, and valuable.

I'm not just talking about parenting. It's a fundamental question that every leader faces today: If AI can analyse data, generate reports, and optimise processes, what makes a human team member valuable? What kind of people do you want on your team, and how do you motivate them in a world where AI can handle the traditional work?

If you're building a team for the next decade, you need people who can do what AI can't. The people you'll want on your team won't just be task completers but culture creators. They won't just deliver results but generate belonging. They'll apply nuance, timing, and ethics to decision-making. They'll ask the right questions, adapt their message to the moment, and listen deeply to understand what's really happening. They'll help others find purpose in their work, role, or contribution–driving motivation, retention, and cultural alignment. Most importantly, they balance strategic thinking with empathy and human impact awareness, ensuring that technology, policy, and product choices remain people-first. They'll be your relational infrastructure.

But here's what's interesting: The things that motivate this new kind of team are different from what motivated previous generations. My generation was largely motivated by clear career progression, financial security, and recognition for individual achievement. We wanted to climb ladders, accumulate credentials, and demonstrate competence through task completion. There might be one or two who disagree; the rest are lying.

The people who thrive in today's workplaces are motivated by different things: the opportunity to make a meaningful impact, the chance to develop uniquely human skills, the satisfaction of creating genuine connections, and the purpose that comes from work that can't be automated. They want to be part of organisations that use AI to amplify human potential not replace it. They want to work for leaders who understand that efficiency without empathy is unsustainable. And they want roles where their creativity, judgement, and relationship-building abilities are valued alongside their technical skills.

This is why retention strategies will change dramatically. Businesses won't keep these people just by offering higher salaries or better benefits. They'll keep them by creating environments where people can do work that matters, where their uniquely human contributions are recognised and developed, where they feel connected to something larger than individual tasks.

This also means hiring differently, training differently, and structuring work differently. We're not just looking for people who can complete tasks but people who can nurture RI. The job descriptions of the future will include requirements like the ability to read unstated client concerns, adapting communication style to different cultural contexts, and building trust across virtual relationships.

But hiring is just the beginning. We also need to create development programs that help people understand how to use AI to enhance their human judgement. Programs such as how to interpret data insights within relational contexts, how to build trust across digital channels, and how to create meaningful connections at scale.

Most importantly, we need to create measurement systems that value relationship building alongside task completion. If we only measure efficiency metrics, we'll optimise away the very human elements that create sustainable success.

Watching Lochlan navigate this changing world gives me hope. His natural curiosity about people, ability to make genuine connections, and instinct for reading what others need aren't skills that AI will make obsolete. They're skills that AI will make more valuable. But I also need to be intentional about helping him develop these capabilities. Just as previous generations needed to learn reading, writing, and arithmetic, this generation needs to learn empathy, creative problem-solving, and complex relationship navigation.

This means encouraging his natural curiosity about people, not just rewarding academic achievement. It means teaching him to ask good questions, listen deeply, and understand perspectives different from his own. It also means helping him see that understanding humans is as important as understanding technology.

When Lochlan comes home talking about the new kid in his class, I encourage him to figure out ways to include him. When he mentions that one of his teachers seems stressed, we talk about what that might mean and how he could help.

When he's frustrated with a friend, we work through understanding the other person's perspective. These sound like character development exercises but they're also future career preparation. The question is whether we'll be wise enough as a society to help kids like Lochlan develop the skills that will make them not just employable but irreplaceable.

# MAPPING YOUR ORGANISATION | 15

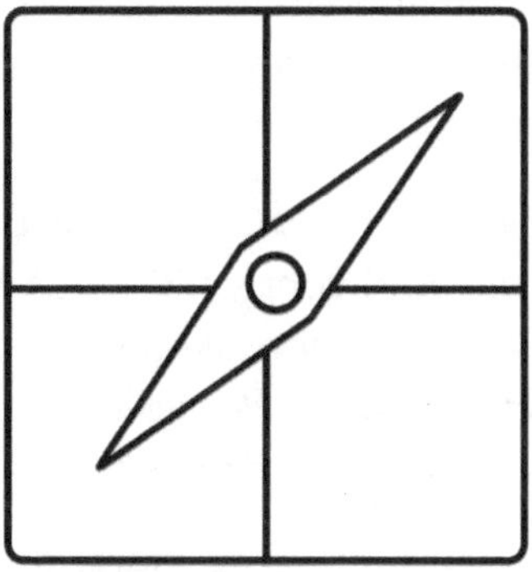

I've worked with two companies in the past that couldn't have been more different–and, in many ways, they became inspiration for me.

The first company prided itself on precision. They were obsessed with process streamlining, optimising, and refining. Everything had a playbook. Their teams were exceptionally good at repeatable tasks, and their operations ran like clockwork. They could present charts and metrics for every possible scenario. I found this difficult because people were rarely allowed outside the system.

The second company was the complete opposite. They focused almost entirely on relationships. They knew their clients deeply, be it birthdays, kids' names, or favourite restaurants. They were warm, thoughtful, and genuinely human in everything they did. But operationally, they struggled. Projects slipped. Deliverables lacked structure. The charm was there, but the rigour wasn't. They often survived only because they were liked.

Over time, I started to see a pattern. When we went into pitches, the process-driven company would lead with efficiency. They'd impress clients with their operational excellence until another team came in with *both* efficiency *and* empathy. When that happened, we lost.

Meanwhile, the relationship-led company excelled in industries that valued creativity and connection, but when pitching to sectors that required precision, like finance, healthcare, and logistics, we couldn't compete. We showed up with warmth and authenticity but not enough discipline or proof of consistency.

What I realised through those experiences was that both companies had mastered part of the equation. One had **high AI but low RI**: brilliant systems, limited soul. The other had **high RI but low AI**: incredible warmth, little structure. Neither could sustain long-term success because both were out of balance.

The companies that consistently won, the ones that clients stayed loyal to, were the ones that had both. They were operationally excellent and emotionally intelligent. They were the companies that used technology to create time and space for human connection, not to replace it.

Noticing this, I began to think more deeply about how to measure and balance these two forces to help organisations intentionally evolve toward a place where process and personality, logic and empathy, technology and trust could coexist. That thinking became the foundation for what I now call the *RI/AI Balance Compass*.

Since the age of AI dawned, some companies have raced toward AI adoption, convinced that technological sophistication alone will create a competitive advantage. Others have resisted automation entirely, believing that human relationships are incompatible with AI. Both approaches miss the bigger picture.

That's why I developed a simple tool to help leaders understand where their organisation currently sits and, more importantly, where it needs to go to thrive in an AI-enhanced world. I call it the RI/AI Balance Compass as it balances RI with AI. As you might imagine for a compass, it's a 2x2 framework that maps organisations based on their development in the two critical areas.

**RI/AI Balance**

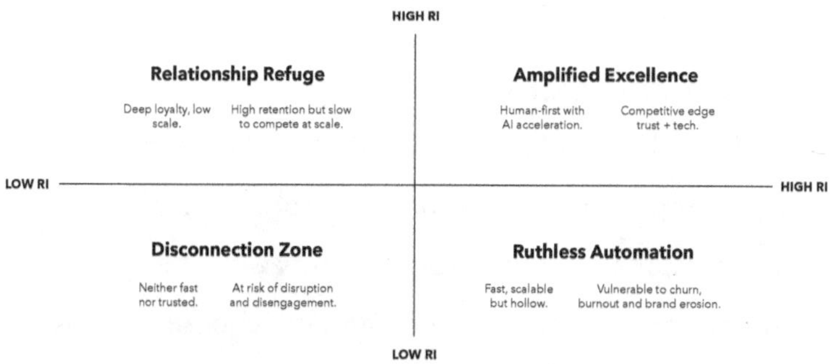


**X-Axis, AI Capability:** This measures how effectively a company leverages automation, data analytics, and artificial intelligence to drive scale, efficiency, and innovation. It ranges from low AI (minimal automation, basic systems) to high AI (sophisticated AI integration across operations).

**Y-Axis, RI Capability:** This measures the depth and quality of human connection across the organisation, such as trust between team members, empathy in customer interactions, effectiveness of communication, and overall psychological safety. It ranges from low RI (transactional relationships, poor communication) to high RI (deep trust, authentic connections, strong loyalty).

Together, these axes create four distinct quadrants, each representing a different strategic position with its own opportunities and risks.

## Disconnection Zone (Low AI/Low RI):

*Neither trusted nor efficient*

Organisations in this quadrant struggle on both sides. They haven't invested in modern technology systems and have failed to build strong relationships with customers or employees. These companies are typically in survival mode, dealing with operational challenges, low morale, and a declining market position.

### Typical Characteristics:

- Outdated technology stack with manual processes
- High employee turnover and low engagement
- Transactional customer relationships with little loyalty
- Poor internal communication and collaboration
- Reactive rather than strategic decision-making

**The risk:** Companies in this zone are exposed on all fronts. They're vulnerable to disruption, struggle with talent retention, and often find themselves competing solely on price, a race they're unlikely to win.

**The opportunity:** While the situation is challenging, companies here have the advantage of being able to build both AI capability and RI simultaneously, creating a strong foundation for sustainable growth.

Consider a traditional manufacturing company that has underinvested for years. Their production systems are decades old, their customer service is purely reactive, and employee morale is low. Transformation here requires parallel investment in both technology and relationships, but if they commit within two years, they can move into a different quadrant and even become a regional leader.

Companies here need to invest in both areas simultaneously, but they should start with RI. It's easier to add technology to strong relationships than to add relationships to impersonal technology.

## Relationship Refuge (Low AI/High RI): *Loyal but lagging*

These organisations have built strong human connections but haven't embraced the technological tools that could amplify their capabilities. They often have excellent company culture, loyal customers, and strong community ties, but they struggle to scale efficiently or compete with more technologically advanced competitors.

### Typical Characteristics:

- Strong organisational culture with high employee loyalty
- Deep customer relationships built on trust and personal service
- Resistance to automation for fear of losing the human touch
- Manual processes that limit scalability
- Competitive disadvantage in speed and efficiency

**The risk:** While these companies enjoy strong relationships, they may find it increasingly difficult to compete as customer expectations evolve and competitors leverage AI for better service delivery.

**The opportunity:** Companies in this quadrant have the hardest part figured out: They know how to build trust and maintain relationships. Adding AI capabilities can amplify these strengths without diminishing them.

Consider a traditional family-owned business that has thrived for generations on personal relationships and community trust. They resist technology because they fear it will compromise what makes them special. But the smart ones are learning that AI can help them provide more personalised service at a greater scale.

These companies should embrace AI as an amplifier of their existing strengths. The key is implementing technology that enhances the human elements that customers value.

## Ruthless Automation (High AI/Low RI):

*Fast and scalable, but emotionally hollow*

Businesses in this quadrant ruthlessly adopt AI and automation but often lose sight of the human elements that drive long-term success. They are efficient and scalable, but they struggle with employee burnout, customer churn, and brand loyalty.

### Typical Characteristics:

- Heavy automation across most business functions
- Impersonal customer service with minimal human interaction
- High-efficiency metrics but declining satisfaction scores

- Internal pressure to optimise everything for speed and cost
- Difficulty building lasting relationships with customers or employees

**The risk:** While these companies may achieve short-term efficiency gains, they're vulnerable to competitors who can match their technological capabilities while providing a superior human experience.

**The opportunity:** Companies here have proven they can implement technology effectively. The challenge is learning to use that technology to enhance rather than substitute human connection.

Consider a tech-first agency that has achieved 90% automation. Their systems are technically impressive, but client relationships are deteriorating because every interaction feels mechanical and impersonal. The solution for them isn't to remove technology but redesign it to support human relationship building.

Companies here need to rebuild the human connections they've optimised away. This often means redesigning processes to include meaningful human touchpoints and training teams to use technology to enhance customer relationships.

## Amplified Excellence (High AI/High RI): *Human-first and AI-powered*

This is the sweet spot where organisations learn to combine technological sophistication with RI. They use AI to handle tasks while freeing humans to focus on relationship building, creative problem-solving, and complex decision-making.

## Typical Characteristics:

- Personalised experiences delivered at scale
- Empowered employees who use AI tools to enhance their capabilities
- Efficient systems that create more time for meaningful human interactions
- Strong customer loyalty combined with operational excellence
- Innovation that serves both efficiency and relationship goals

**The opportunity:** Companies in this quadrant have sustainable competitive advantages that are difficult for competitors to replicate. They compete on trust, insight, and value creation rather than just price and features.

**The challenge:** Maintaining this balance requires ongoing attention and strategic discipline. It's easy to drift towards pure efficiency optimisation when under pressure.

Consider a consultancy that has landed in this quadrant by being intentional about using AI to amplify its human capabilities. They've learned that the goal isn't to choose between efficiency and relationships but to use technology in service of both.

Companies here must resist the constant pressure to optimise away human elements. The goal is maintaining the balance while continuously improving both technological and relational capabilities.

## Where Does Your Organisation Live?

Most leaders I work with can immediately identify which quadrant describes their organisation. But here are some diagnostic questions to help clarify your position:

### AI Capability Assessment:

- How much of your routine work is automated?
- Do you use data analytics to inform strategic decisions?
- Can your systems adapt and learn from experience?
- Are your employees empowered with AI tools that enhance their capabilities?

### RI Assessment:

- Do customers choose you primarily for relationships or just for features and pricing?
- How would your employees describe the culture and communication within your organisation?
- When problems arise, do stakeholders trust your organisation to handle them fairly?
- Do your processes feel supportive or bureaucratic to the people who interact with them?

Understanding your current position can help you make better decisions about where to invest and how to evolve. The question every leader must answer is: What are you doing to move toward amplified excellence?

As AI capabilities become democratised across industries, every company will have access to similar AI tools. The competitive advantage will belong to organisations that can combine those tools with superior human connection.

Companies stuck in the lower quadrants face increasing pressure. Those optimising for efficiency alone will find themselves in a race to the bottom, competing primarily on price. Those relying solely on relationships without technological enhancement will struggle to scale and innovate.

Companies that reach amplified excellence are positioning themselves for sustainable success. There, they can compete on trust, insight, and value creation, areas where human-AI collaboration creates advantages that pure technology or pure relationships cannot achieve alone. Now, it's time to implement it.

# IMPLEMENTING BALANCE | 16

The question I get most often from people who understand the importance of RI is: "This all makes sense, but how do I implement it? How do I build these skills while still getting my work done?"

It's a fair question. In theory, everyone agrees that relationships matter. In practice, most people feel too busy, overwhelmed, or focused on immediate deadlines to invest the time and energy that relationships require.

The solution isn't to completely overhaul how you work but make small, strategic adjustments that compound over time. Rather than trying to master all aspects of RI at once, focus on developing one signal at a time while gradually integrating them into your daily workflow.

## Signal 1: Awareness (The 3-minute check-in)

**The practice:** Start every interaction with three minutes dedicated to reading the room. This isn't small talk but strategic intelligence-gathering about the human dynamics that affect everything else.

I start every one-on-one meeting with a genuine check-in: "What's on your mind this week? What's going well? What's challenging?" Not to be polite–I'm actively reading for:

- Contradictions between what someone says and how they say it
- Energy shifts that indicate stress, excitement, or disengagement
- Timing signals that suggest when to push forward versus pull back

I learn more about my team's actual capacity and concerns from these three minutes than from any status report. If someone seems overwhelmed, I adjust my approach for the rest of the conversation. If someone seems excited about something, I explore opportunities to leverage that enthusiasm.

### Implementation Tools:

- Block out the first 3-5 minutes of every meeting for relationship intelligence
- Create a mental checklist:
    - What's their energy level?
    - What's their emotional state?
    - What's different from usual?
- Adjust your agenda based on what you observe

## Signal 2: Presence (Introduce digital boundaries)

**The practice:** Maintain full connection in the moment by creating systems that eliminate digital distractions and enable complete attention. I call this the *presence protocol*. (I've been forced as part of this book to title some concepts that sound fluffy. I apologise.)

When someone comes to the office or joins a virtual meeting:

- Close the laptop or turn away from your screen
- Put your phone away
- Make eye contact during important points and give them your full attention
- Ask one opening question and then truly listen to the answer

### Implementation Tools:

- Create phone-free zones for important conversations
- Use the presence pause–three seconds of full attention before responding
- Practice the looping technique: Reflect what you heard before adding your own thoughts

## Signal 3: Empathic Structuring (Introduce a care-framework system)

**The practice:** Build care and boundaries into your work processes from the beginning, creating frameworks that balance support with accountability.

I have systematised an approach that includes:

- **Communication preferences:** How does this person like to receive feedback? What's their decision-making style?
- **Support structures:** What does accountability look like for them? What kind of check-ins are most helpful?
- **Boundary clarification:** What are their stress signals? When do they need space versus support?

### Implementation Tools:

- Create onboarding templates that include emotional and working style preferences
- Design feedback systems that address both task completion and relationship health
- Build regular relationship check-ins into project timelines

## Signal 4: Connection Capital (Invest in compound returns)

**The practice:** Systematically invest in relationships that compound over time through regular, non-transactional interactions and proactive value-sharing.

Remember the 3-2-1 relationship investment system from earlier? As a reminder, offer:

- 3 non-transactional touchpoints per quarter with key relationships
- 2 pieces of valuable content shared proactively (articles, introductions, insights)
- 1 personal milestone remembered and acknowledged

### Implementation Tools:

- Create a customer relationship management system that tracks personal information, concerns, and follow-up actions
- Schedule quarterly relationship reviews, not just business reviews
- Develop a value-first mindset: Always ask what you can give before what you can get

## Signal 5: Human Differentiation (Deliver authentic judgement)

**The practice:** Bring uniquely human qualities to your leadership by leveraging intuition, creative problem-solving, and values-based judgement in ways that AI cannot replicate.

I'm known for being brutally honest, and here is what I use:

- Intuition from lived experience about what will and won't work
- Creative approaches that break established patterns
- Authentic vulnerability about limitations and capabilities
- Values-based judgement that prioritises long-term relationship health over short-term profit

### Implementation Tools:

- Develop decision frameworks that include both logical and emotional considerations
- Practice authentic vulnerability by admitting limitations and uncertainties
- Create space for intuitive judgement alongside data-driven analysis
- Build values-based criteria for major decisions

Now I know what you're thinking. Is she serious? This is common sense! And indeed, it is, but are you using your common sense intentionally? The biggest challenge in implementing the five skills is making it sustainable. It's easy to do this for a few weeks when you're motivated but harder to maintain as a consistent practice.

The key is to integrate these signals into your existing workflows rather than treating them as additional tasks.

**Daily Integration:**

- Morning: Review your calendar and identify which signal will be most important for each interaction
- During meetings: Use the awareness check-in to calibrate your approach
- Evening: Reflect on relationship moments and plan follow-up actions

**Weekly Integration:**

- Monday: Review your connection capital investments for the week.
- Wednesday: Check in on empathic structuring–are your frameworks working?
- Friday: Assess your human differentiation moments–where did you bring unique value?

**Monthly Integration:**

- Review relationship health metrics alongside business metrics
- Adjust your approach based on what's working and what isn't
- Plan deeper connection capital investments for the following month

Traditional business metrics don't capture RI well, but you can track leading indicators that suggest your skills are strengthening.

## Awareness Indicators:

- Fewer surprises in meetings (you're reading the room better)
- More proactive problem-solving (you're catching issues earlier)
- Better timing of requests and proposals

## Presence Indicators:

- Deeper conversations in the same amount of time
- People sharing more sensitive information with you
- Increased energy and engagement in your interactions

## Empathic Structuring Indicators:

- Fewer relationship breakdowns and misunderstandings
- More efficient conflict resolution
- Higher satisfaction with collaborative processes

## Connection Capital Indicators:

- Increased referrals and recommendations
- More unsolicited contact from your network
- Longer, more strategic conversations with key relationships

### Human Differentiation Indicators:

- Being asked for advice on issues beyond your technical expertise
- Inclusion in strategic conversations and decision-making
- Recognition of creative or innovative approaches

The most important measurement is qualitative: Are your relationships becoming more trusted, more collaborative, and more mutually beneficial over time?

# THE RELATIONSHIP-FIRST COMPANY | 17

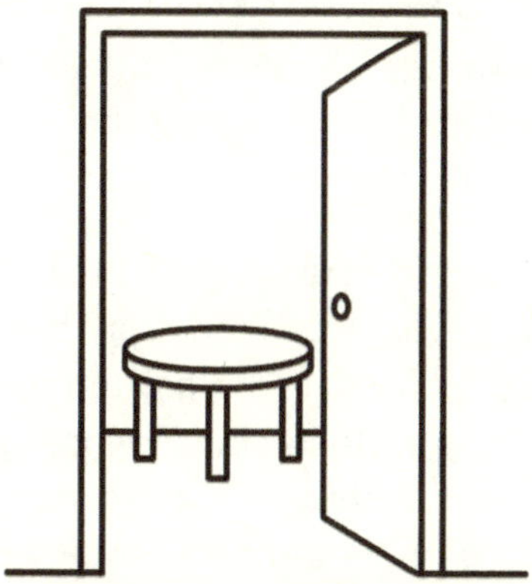

I've been paying close attention to companies since the age of AI because I want to understand how they deal with the five signals of RI. Not that they are calling it that, of course.

What I've seen is struggling companies optimise everything for efficiency, using AI to minimise human touchpoints. Thriving ones use the same AI tools to create more space for human connection. If the lesson isn't clear yet: AI can make you more efficient, but only relationships can make you more valuable. That's why we have to lead by being relationship-first, not least because AI can do the broad parts faster, while relationships take longer to build.

Creating a relationship-first company means systematically developing each of the five skills at an organisational level, and building them into your culture, processes, and technology systems.

## Signal 1: Organisational Awareness

Companies with strong awareness capabilities don't just track metrics–they read the human signals that predict changes in market conditions, team performance, and client satisfaction.

This means leadership that reads the room by paying attention to energy levels in meetings, contradictions between what teams say and how they act, and timing around major decisions. It means implementing customer intelligence systems that track emotional and relationship indicators, not just transaction data. It also means implementing employee engagement approaches that focus on early warning signals rather than just annual survey results.

A mid-sized consulting firm restructured its account management approach around organisational awareness. Instead of quarterly business reviews focused solely on metrics, they implemented monthly relationship intelligence sessions where account managers shared observations about changes in client communication patterns, shifts in stakeholder influence and decision-making, and emerging concerns that haven't yet become formal issues. This way, they were able to address relationship issues before they became business problems.

## Signal 2: Organisational Presence

Companies with strong presence capabilities design their physical and digital environments to support meaningful human connection, not just operational efficiency.

This includes designing meetings that prioritise relationship building alongside task completion, office layouts that encourage spontaneous interaction and collaboration, technology systems that enhance human connection, and calendar cultures that protect time for relationship-building activities.

A software company redesigned its entire service delivery model around presence principles. They use AI to handle routine customer support tasks, but every client also has a dedicated relationship manager who conducts monthly strategic conversations not just problem-solving, maintains full presence during client interactions (with no multitasking), and creates personalised approaches based on each client's communication preferences. As a result, customer satisfaction scores increased.

## Signal 3: Organisational Empathic Structuring

Companies with strong empathic structuring in place build care and boundaries into their operational frameworks, creating systems that balance support with accountability.

This means implementing hiring processes that evaluate empathic capability alongside technical skills, performance management that includes relationship health metrics, client onboarding processes that establish working agreements and communication preferences, and feedback systems that address both task completion and relationship quality.

A professional services firm redesigned its project management methodology around empathic structuring. Every project now includes client work-style assessment and adaptation, regular relationship health check-ins alongside project status updates, structured feedback loops that address both deliverables and collaboration experience, and clear escalation paths for relationship issues, not just technical problems. As a result, their project success rates sky-rocketed.

## Signal 4: Organisational Connection Capital

Companies with strong connection capital capabilities systematically invest in relationships that compound over time, treating relationship health as a strategic asset.

This includes implementing CRM systems that track relationship depth not just transaction history, account management focused on long-term value creation rather than short-term revenue optimisation, network development that creates mutual value across the entire business ecosystem, and knowledge systems that capture and share relationship intelligence across the whole company.

An accounting firm transformed its business model around connection capital principles. In doing so, they limited client roster size to enable deeper relationships, invested in understanding each client's strategic context not just their immediate needs, created systematic approaches to non-transactional value-sharing, and built relationship health metrics into their performance evaluation system. By doing this, their average client relationship value increased while client acquisition costs decreased–win-win!

## Signal 5: Organisational Human Differentiation

Companies with strong human differentiation capabilities position themselves around the uniquely human value they provide, using AI to amplify that.

This means designing services that emphasise creative problem-solving and strategic thinking; value propositions based on trust, judgement, and relationship quality; technology that creates more space for human connection, and a culture that celebrates uniquely human capabilities.

A consulting firm repositioned its entire value proposition around human differentiation. To do this, they used AI to handle data analysis and routine research; focused human efforts on strategic interpretation, creative problem-solving, and relationship building; emphasised values-based judgement and intuitive insights in their client work; and built their brand around trusted adviser relationships rather than technical expertise. As a result, they were able to raise prices while increasing demand because clients value the uniquely human elements of their service.

The most successful companies don't just implement these signals individually–they integrate them into a system where each signal reinforces the others. In these companies, senior executives create cultures where these capabilities are developed and rewarded. They design AI systems to enhance human connection, creating time and space for relationship building. They implement metrics that track relationship health alongside operational efficiency, creating accountability for long-term value creation. They build hiring, development, and performance management systems that prioritise RI alongside technical capabilities.

Companies that master the five skills create sustainable competitive advantages that are difficult for competitors to replicate for various reasons. Their premium positioning is based on trust and relationship quality rather than just technical capability. They attract the best talent as people prefer to work for companies that value human connection. Their network effects compound over time as relationships create referrals and collaborative opportunities. And they are more resilient during market downturns because strong relationships provide stability.

The choice we make about how to balance AI capabilities with RI will shape the next several decades of human experience. We can create a future where AI amplifies our humanity or where it systematically erodes the relationships that make life meaningful.

The round table taught me that everyone has something valuable to contribute, but not everyone will be heard unless someone makes the effort to listen. In our AI-enhanced future, that effort–the choice to develop RI–will be what separates companies that thrive from those that merely survive.

It's the differentiator for whether the organisations we build achieve amplified excellence–the sweet spot where high AI capability meets high RI–or whether they'll drift into ruthless automation where efficiency without empathy creates systems that are fast but hollow.

It's time to choose. Not just for our businesses, but for the next generation watching us navigate this transition. The future of human connection depends on it.

# CONCLUSION:
## The Amplified Future

I'm writing this on a Thursday evening while Lochlan, Grayson, Willow, and Cooper are scattered around the house–Lochlan using AI to research his latest obsession with marine biology, Grayson building something impossibly complex with Lego, Willow organising her stuffed animals into what she insists is a very important meeting, and Cooper finding joy in absolutely everything.

As I watch them, I don't see a dark future where machines replace human connection. I see what I've always seen, from that round table to the stroke ward during COVID: humans finding ways to connect, care, and create meaning together, using whatever tools are available to amplify their humanity. The future isn't something that happens to us. It's something we choose, conversation by conversation, relationship by relationship, decision by decision.

In that classroom in 1989, the teacher thought she was organising us by ability, but what she did was create the perfect conditions for us to develop the skills that would matter most forty years later. We couldn't compete using traditional metrics, but we excelled at less measurable metrics like reading people, building trust, and finding creative solutions.

Now AI is putting everyone at the round table. The square and triangle table skills like processing information quickly, following standard procedures, and executing tasks efficiently are what AI does best. But the round table skills like understanding what people really need, adapting to different personalities, and creating genuine connection are becoming the most valuable capabilities in the world.

Thankfully, this isn't a threat; it's a liberation. Just as AI helped me overcome my dyslexia to write this book, it can help all of us overcome our individual limitations to focus on what makes us most human. It can help individuals and companies amplify what they do best: humans helping other humans.

My father walked the streets of Manorhamilton checking on senior residents not because it was efficient but because he understood that community safety came from human connection.

My mother sat with patients in Sligo General, providing not just medical care but presence. She didn't have AI to handle the routine tasks, so she had to squeeze relationship building into the margins of overwhelming workloads.

Imagine if they'd had AI as their partner. Dad could have used it to analyse crime patterns and coordinate resources, freeing him up to spend even more time building relationships that were his real crime prevention system. He'd still throw those Christmas parties for seniors, but AI would help him identify who was becoming isolated, who needed extra support, who might be at risk.

Mum could have used AI to handle medication calculations and treatment protocols, creating more time for conversations that addressed patients' fears and hopes. She'd still notice when someone needed extra reassurance, but AI would help her track recovery patterns and identify when someone needed that human touch most.

This is the inheritance we're creating for our children–not a world where technology replaces human connection, but one where it amplifies our capacity to care.

William didn't just run a haulage company–he built a network of relationships where every delivery was an opportunity to understand and serve human needs better. The bride whose wedding dress he personally ensured arrived safely became a customer for life. Not because of the efficiency of the delivery, but because of the humanity of the service.

In our AI-amplified future, every business has the potential to operate like William's–using technology to handle logistics while focusing human energy on understanding and serving the deeper needs that create lasting loyalty.

The tea lady who sat with me when I was separated from six-day-old Willow didn't have an algorithm telling her what to do. She had something more powerful: the human ability to recognise suffering and choose to respond with kindness. She could have efficiently served tea and moved on. Instead, she chose to create a moment of human connection that I'll remember forever.

And this is what's beautiful about our future: AI can handle the tea service, the scheduling, the logistics, the documentation–and this means more people can focus on being present for the moments that matter, like sitting with a scared mother, sharing stories that provide comfort, creating the human connections that help us heal.

The radiologist who stayed late to help get me back to Willow didn't do it because a system told her to. She did it because one mother recognised another mother's need. In the future, AI can handle the routine scans, the standard cases–freeing up radiologists to focus on the complex cases and the human moments that require judgement, empathy, and wisdom.

The Reserve Army and its buddy system, where our success is interconnected, and we rise or fall together. Sinéad and I supported each other not because we were ordered to, but because the system made mutual support the natural response.

Imagine this principle applied everywhere and amplified by AI, like schools where AI tracks learning patterns while humans provide mentorship and emotional support. Every child could have both technological assistance and human champions who see their unique potential, like those of us at the round table needed.

Workplaces where AI handles task coordination while humans focus on collaboration and creativity. Every team member could have both efficient systems and genuine relationships that help them thrive.

Communities where AI identifies needs while humans provide care. Every person could have both systematic support and authentic connection.

Leah at Terry's Youth Centre showed me what systematic care looks like–structure that serves human needs rather than constraining them. She created frameworks that addressed both practical necessities and emotional realities.

This is the model for our amplified future: AI handles the framework while humans provide the care. AI can track schedules, manage resources, and coordinate logistics. But humans decide how to adapt those systems to individual needs, respond when someone is struggling, celebrate when someone succeeds. Every organisation could operate like Terry's, using technology to create efficiency while maintaining flexibility and humanity.

Here's what I know: We get to choose. Just as the round table kids chose to develop different skills when traditional paths were closed to them, rather than choosing to give up, we can choose how to use AI in service of human connection. We can say "to hell with it all" and give in, or we can choose to lean into what we can do and develop strengths to get around our challenges.

We can choose to be like the partner who used AI to automate everything and lost the relationships that mattered–or we can choose to use AI to create more space for those relationships.

We can choose to optimise for efficiency alone–or we can choose amplified excellence, where efficiency serves relationship building.

We can choose to see AI as a replacement for human capabilities–or we can choose to see it as an amplifier that helps us overcome limitations and focus on what makes us most human.

When I watch Lochlan navigate his school, knowing everyone from the milk delivery person to the principal, I don't see someone who'll be replaced by AI. I see someone who understands intuitively what I learned at the round table–that human connection is the real currency of success.

When Grayson builds his elaborate Lego creations, I see the same creative problem-solving that no algorithm can replicate–the ability to envision something that doesn't exist and bring it into being through patience and imagination.

When Willow organises her stuffed animals into very important meetings, I see the early development of the organisational and relational skills that will help her create structures that serve human needs.

When Cooper finds joy in everything, I see the emotional intelligence that will help him bring light to whatever darkness the future might hold.

They're growing up native to both AI and human connection. They don't see these as opposing forces but as natural partners. Lochlan uses AI to research marine biology, then excitedly shares what he's learned with anyone who'll listen, creating human connection through technological capability.

This is their inheritance–not a world where they must choose between efficiency and empathy, but one where technology amplifies their capacity for both.

In many ways, AI is bringing us full circle. For decades, we've optimised for efficiency, standardisation, and measurement. We built systems that often worked against human nature rather than with it. We relegated relationship building to the margins, treating it as a nice-to-have rather than essential infrastructure.

But AI is forcing us to remember what really matters. When machines can handle routine tasks better than humans, the only sustainable advantage is being more human–more creative, more empathetic, more capable of the complex relationship navigation that builds trust and creates meaning.

Human connection isn't just a nice-to-have. It's the foundation of everything worthwhile. So, here's my promise to my children, and to yours.

We won't let AI diminish your humanity. But instead, we'll use it to amplify your unique gifts, to overcome your individual limitations, to create more space for the relationships and creativity that make life meaningful.

We'll build organisations that value your ability to connect, care, and create–not just your ability to process and produce.

We'll create educational systems that develop your RI as systematically as your technical skills, knowing that both are essential for the future you'll inhabit.

We'll design technologies that serve human flourishing rather than replacing human connection, that bring us together rather than driving us apart.

The future isn't about humans versus AI. It's about humans with AI, amplified and empowered to be more connected, creative, and capable of building the kind of world where everyone has a seat at the table–preferably a round one, where nobody will get hurt on the corners and everyone can see each other equally.

This is the future I see when I watch my children. They won't have to choose between technology and humanity. They'll use both to build something we can barely imagine–a world where AI handles the routine so humans can focus on the remarkable. Where efficiency serves relationships rather than replacing them, and the skills developed in situations like at my round table everywhere become the foundation for what I call amplified excellence.

It's not just hope–it's a choice. And one we can make, starting right now, in every interaction, relationship, and decision.

I believe we will. Because in the end, we're still those kids at the round table, finding ways to connect, contribute, and matter. Finally, we have the tools to build a world where everyone's unique contribution is not just valued but amplified.

That's the future we're choosing. The inheritance we're creating. And the story we're writing together. It's going to be beautiful.

# APPENDIX 1

# The Path Forward: Quick List

In this book, we've looked at the path forward through five core signals. Here is a quick list of the core signals for individuals, businesses, and society. You may wish to map these to your own life or company.

## The Individual Path: Developing Your 5 Signals

If you're an individual who wants to become more skilled at human connection, the path forward requires you to develop each signal systematically.

### Awareness:

- Practice reading rooms and noticing contradictions between what people say and how they say it
- Develop timing instincts for when to push forward versus pull back
- Create systems for gathering and acting on emotional intelligence

## Presence:

- Eliminate digital distractions during important conversations
- Practice giving your full attention and active listening
- Learn to make others feel truly seen and heard

## Empathic Structuring:

- Build care and boundaries into your work processes
- Create frameworks that balance support with accountability
- Design feedback systems that address both tasks and relationships

## Connection Capital:

- Invest in relationships that compound over time
- Practice non-transactional value-sharing
- Build systematic approaches to relationship maintenance

## Human Differentiation:

- Leverage your intuition and lived experience
- Develop creative approaches that break established patterns
- Practice authentic vulnerability and values-based judgement

## The Organisational Path: Building 5-Signal Systems

If you're a leader who wants to build a better company, the path forward requires systematic development of each skill.

**Cultural foundation:** Leadership that models all five signals and creates systems that reward RI alongside technical capability.

**Technology integration:** AI deployment that amplifies human connection, creating more space for relationship building.

**Talent systems:** Hiring, development, and performance management that prioritises RI.

**Service design:** Value propositions based on relationship quality and uniquely human capabilities.

**Measurement systems:** Metrics that track relationship health alongside operational efficiency.

## The Societal Path: Creating 5-Signal Communities

If you're someone who cares about the society we're creating, the path forward requires building the five skills into our social infrastructure:

**Educational systems:** Teaching RI as systematically as we teach technical skills.

**Workplace design:** Creating environments that support human connection and collaborative problem-solving.

**Technology governance:** Ensuring that AI deployment serves human flourishing rather than replacing meaningful interaction.

**Cultural values:** Celebrating people and organisations that excel at human connection.

# APPENDIX 2

## Pattern Recognition: Quick List

In chapter 9, we looked at pattern recognition, and looking back at my career, I could see how the same pattern recognition abilities transferred across completely different contexts. I'll add a quick list of them here, and you may wish to do the same to notice how the patterns from your earlier experiences map to workplace scenarios.

From the round table to client management:

- Reading teacher moods → Reading client stress signals
- Understanding what classmates really needed → Understanding what clients want beyond their stated requirements
- Adapting to different personalities → Customising communication styles for different stakeholders

From community policing, observing my father, to business development:

- Building trust with community members → Building trust with business partners
- Understanding the broader context of people's concerns → Understanding the strategic context of business challenges

- Maintaining relationships during difficult periods → Managing partnerships through market changes

From military service to team leadership:

- The buddy system approach → Collaborative accountability in business teams
- Reading group dynamics during training → Understanding team dynamics during projects
- Balancing individual needs with collective objectives → Balancing client needs with business sustainability

From charity work to organisational design:

- Creating sustainable care systems → Building scalable client success processes
- Managing cross-cultural collaboration → Managing diverse stakeholder relationships
- Balancing idealism with practical constraints → Balancing vision with operational realities

# ACKNOWLEDGEMENTS

There are so many people who have helped me along the way as I developed this concept–particularly colleagues and friends–far too many to mention individually.

However, there are two people I want to call out in particular: Angie O'Dowd and Kate Lesniak. From the very beginning, they gave me the belief and encouragement I needed, and their support was instrumental in giving me the confidence to share this idea with the world for the first time.

I would also like to thank the McDevitt and Duffy families, who feature so heavily in this book. Thank you for all of your support throughout my childhood–I am truly grateful.

To my siblings, my mother Delia, and the Stone family–thank you for your constant support and encouragement.

Finally, none of this would have been possible without my darling wife, Geraldine, and our four beautiful children, Lochlan, Grayson, Willow, and Cooper. Thank you for always believing in me and for giving me the support and courage to make this possible.

# ABOUT THE AUTHOR

**Sarah Stone McDevitt** is a senior SaaS professional and a leading voice on the intersection of technology and human connection. She has spent her career working in partner ecosystems and is the creator of Relational Intelligence–a framework shaping how organisations design hybrid teams, build trust, and adopt AI responsibly.

Raised in Sligo, Ireland, Sarah is the daughter of a Garda sergeant and a hospital nurse–two professions grounded in care, trust, and human understanding. As one of four siblings, she learned early that success depends not just on what you know, but how well you understand people.

Now based in Dublin with her wife and their four children, Sarah believes that relationships are the foundation of every meaningful outcome. Her work centres on a simple but powerful idea: *RI + AI = Trust*. Organisations that use artificial intelligence to amplify–not replace–human connection will build deeper trust and more enduring competitive advantage than technology alone can deliver.

Help this book reach more readers

If you found it valuable, please leave a review on Amazon:

www.ingramcontent.com/pod-product-compliance
Lightning Source LLC
LaVergne TN
LVHW100317210926
848480LV00003B/1158
* 9 7 8 1 7 3 8 4 2 6 2 8 7 *